Hiring, Motivating,
and Retaining
the Employee of
the New Millenium

"Where Did I Put That Cattle Prod?"

Robert K. McIntosh

with a forward by Mark Victor Hansen

Lakeshore Communications, Inc.
Euclid, Ohio

Published by: *Lakeshore Publications*, Div.
Lakeshore Communications Inc.
24100 Lakeshore Blvd.
Euclid, OH 44123
(216) 731-0234
800.537.7054

Printed in the United States of America

B C D E F G E

ISBN 1-893435-040

This publication is designed to provide accurate and authoritative information with regard to the subject matter involved. It is sold with the understanding that the publisher is not engaged in rendering legal, accounting or other professional advice. If legal advice or other expert assistance is required, the services of a qualified professional person should be sought.

-From: **A Declaration of Principles**, jointly adopted by a Committee of the American Bar Association and a Committee of Publishers and Associations.

Visit our home page at: http://www.willese-press.com

"Where Did I Put That Cattle Prod?"

Definition: Cattle Prod

1: A device used for making dumb animals do what you want them to do.

2: Any device used by managers who can't tell the difference between people and dumb animals.

Foreword by Mark Victor Hansen

I love this book! It talks to the heart of every business—its people. It teaches the owner and manager how to succeed in the people business. Employees make or break a business, and Robert teaches you how to be a breakthrough owner-manager-leader.

"Where Did I Put That Cattle Prod?" teaches want-to-be leaders how to become enlightened, visionary leaders. Stories are the best way to communicate from one heart to another; Robert tells crystal clear stories and then edifies you with clear key points. The repetition insures you get, understand, and can use his salient messages.

Robert has mastered 30 years of business wisdom and distilled it into a practical game plan so that you can become monstrously successful-if you're ready and want to.

Enjoy drinking in the insights that will make your life infinitely better in every way.

Happy reading,

Mark Victor Hansen
Creator, Chicken Soup for the Soul

Table of Contents

Introduction

Today's employment environment is radically different from that existing when I opened my first fast food restaurant in 1964. Since then I have owned and operated six different businesses and managed hundreds of employees. Looking back over 35 years of experience, I have learned that the crying need today in business is owners and managers who are skilled at dealing with the employee of the new millennium. And those of us who manage employees must realize that, to a great degree, we are responsible for the performance of our employees. I enjoy the following story that illustrates this point.

A young man was hired to manage a business. He went to a management consultant to get some advice. The consultant gave him three envelopes and told him to open them as he felt the need. The young man worked for three months and the business was not doing very well. A meeting was set with the owner. Before he went to the meeting, he opened the first envelope. He read, "Blame the assistant manager." He did and the owner gave him three more months to turn the business around. At the end of the three months the business was still doing poorly. Another meeting was set with the owner. The young man opened the second envelope. He read, "Blame the employees." He did and the business owner gave him one more chance. After three months, there was still no improvement. So the young man read the final envelope. "Write the same things, put them in three envelopes and give them to your replacement!"

What is different today than it was twenty or thirty years ago that requires us to be better managers?

1. *The labor market has shrunk.*

Today we must be more innovative in finding competent employees to work for us. This is particularly true with regards to the entry-level worker market. Businesses like those in the fast food industry are constantly scrambling to fill positions. In some cases, the only qualification is if the person is breathing! Therefore, the competition for workers is fierce. As someone has said, "It's a war out there!"

With this competition for workers has come an attitude among many employees that if they don't like a particular job they can go right down the street and immediately find another. The statement, "You can take this job and shove it!" is common among many of today's workers.

2. *The quality of potential employees has in some ways declined.*

I have noticed a difference between employees I have hired most recently and those of the 60's. For example, they need more direction, more training, and more supervision. It is also a lot more difficult to motivate them. There is an attitude among many workers today that they are doing us a favor by working for us. I remember in the 60's some of my employees actually thanking me for their job! We must be more skilled today at motivating the employee of the new millennium.

3. The high cost of turnover.

Each time an employee quits or we let one go, we might just as well go to the toilet and flush some money down the drain. How much money? It depends on the industry. Some fast food chains estimate a loss of $1000 to $1500 for each terminated employee. Given the time and effort spent in training and the impact on customer satisfaction, that figure could be considerably higher. My experience is that it takes at least one to three months to properly train an employee. Therefore, retention of good employees is absolutely essential.

4. The increase in workplace litigation.

Thirty years ago I never thought that I might be sued by one of my employees or customers. Today it is not a question of if we will be sued, but when. Lawsuits range from sexual harassment to Workman's Compensation claims. The problem with a lawsuit is that no one really wins except the lawyers! For this reason, business owners and managers today must constantly cover their rear end.

There are a number of other differences between employees today and those I hired in the 60's, but these four seem to be the most significant. What I have learned over these past thirty years is simply this: business owners and managers of this new millennium must be better prepared and skilled than ever before. Those of us who manage people must become more than managers. We must become *Leaders*. The word manage comes from the word manos, which means to handle. Managers handle things. They handle operational things such as payroll, reports, ordering of inventory, and advertising. Each of these items are very important. The root word of leader is lead. A Leader leads people. Leaders are concerned about the development of their employees and people follow them because they want to. I have the firm belief that no one is really born to be a business leader. Leadership requires the type of skills that can be acquired only through experience, observation, reflection, and a willingness to learn and to change. Business owners and managers must balance operations and leadership. Most managers have found that leadership is the most difficult of the two. And today, a "Cattle Prod Mentality" won't cut it! The purpose of this book is to examine how managers can become leaders by offering suggestions as to how to hire, motivate, and retain the employee of the new millennium.

Throughout the book, from now on, I will use the word "coworker" instead of employee. The reason is that "coworker" communicates my philosophy that we should consider those we manage as our partners in the business. I have consistently used the first person "I" because of the experiences I have personally had managing coworkers. Each chapter begins with a principle that forms the basis of the chapter. A principle is a single idea that can govern our conduct in a variety of similar situations. For example, "honesty is the best policy" is a principle that has application at home, at work, and in many other situations. This book cannot answer all of the specific situations that will arise in the workplace between manager and coworker. However, when basic principles are understood, they can be applied to the many different situations we face with our coworkers.

The book is divided into three sections.

Section 1- Hiring Coworkers

Section 2- Motivating and Retaining Coworkers

Section 3- Avoiding Costly Litigation

It is my hope that readers of this book will find a few ideas -- or "nuggets" -- that can make the great challenge of leading the worker of this new millennium somewhat easier and more enjoyable. I would like to thank the many coworkers I have had who have taught me so much about leadership. A special thanks to Leonard Tourney of the University of California, Santa Barbara, for his insights and editing of the manuscript. To Dr. Howard Hamilton for his encouragement and advice. To Harvey Turner whose years of management experience added to this book. To Linda Burzynski for her support and encouragement. To John Lovern, friend and mentor. To Roger Williams, friend and publisher. Jim Fedor, for designing the cover. And finally, to Mark Victor Hansen for taking time from his busy schedule to review the manuscript.

SECTION 1

HIRING COWORKERS

Chapter 1

Creatively Finding Employees

Principle: Recruitment is an ongoing marketing effort.

Finding people to hire is as important to a business as recruiting is to a sports team. It is one of those constant challenges that business owners face. I have had many business owners tell me this is the most challenging aspect of their business. Drive down a street in a business district in most any city in America and you will see a proliferation of "Now Hiring" signs. The Employment Opportunity sections of most newspapers are filled with job openings. In today's business environment, attracting good people needs to be a #1 priority.

Consider the benefits when this is done:

- Turnover is not as much of a problem.
- You have people to fill in should there be sickness or absenteeism.
- You experience less stress because you are not so worried about filling positions.

Attracting good employees is like fishing. Fishing requires that you first determine the kind of fish you want to catch. You wouldn't look for trout in the ocean or swordfish in a mountain stream. Second, you select the proper bait and, third, decide where to find the fish. Finally, you have to be able to hook the fish once it bites. These four steps are involved in finding people to hire.

Step 1- Determine the type of people who will be interested in and successful in your type of business.

Each type of business will attract a certain type of person. For example, many franchised businesses hire entry-level workers. Accounting companies usually hire college graduates. There must be a fit between the people you hire and the work they do. An old adage says, "You can't fit a round peg in a square hole." This is an extremely important idea. If you hire someone who can't do the job, you will quickly lose them. I, therefore, develop a profile of the type of person I would ideally like to hire. I look for five characteristics.

- Job capability- Are they able to do what the job requires? Do they have the skills or are they capable of learning them—and quickly?

- Job compatibility- Can the job I am offering them meet their needs? Financially? Schedule wise?

- Personality- Will they fit in with my other team members and my customers? Will their temperament be compatible with the work environment?

- Track record- Have they shown stability and honesty in the past?

- Motivation- Do they really need the job and are they motivated to stick with it?

Step 2- Know where to find the people you want to hire.

Good fishermen know where to find the fish they want. The same principle holds true for the people we want to hire. For example, those who hire entry-level workers need to know where they live, the places they shop, and where they go for recreation. Why is it important to know these things? Today, perhaps more than in the past, we need to be creative in our search efforts. Sometimes it is not enough to just run an ad in the newspaper. When we know where our type of employee is, we can use that knowledge to help us attract future employees. Let me share a couple of examples.

A manager of a senior care facility typically found that non-Caucasian, entry-level workers were his best source of employees. He therefore printed up flyers announcing his job opportunities and hung them in places where his target group was found. For example, he hung flyers in local laundry mats and neighborhood grocery stores. He also made post cards and mailed them to the zip codes where this target audience typically lived. He told me that he always had a reservoir of people from which to hire. Now that's creativity!

Another creative manager told me that to find employees she contacted churches and synagogues, attended local school job fairs, and hung job announcements in local grocery stores. Another used a local newspaper that specifically targeted the people she wanted.

If finding coworkers to hire is a major problem, then one solution is to become creative in the ways you attract people to your business. This may require some research on your part to determine the demographics of your area.

Step 3- Know how to "hook" them.

Employers sometimes make the mistake of baiting the hook with their own favorite bait, such as advancement opportunities and benefits. What is better is to select the bait appropriate to their target group.

For example, a few years ago I conducted a survey of entry-level workers to determine what they wanted in a job. I learned that three of their most important needs were:

- Flexible hours.
- Enough money to cover living expenses.
- A positive work environment.

I learned that entry-level workers were not usually concerned as much about advancement opportunities as they were about immediate cash. Each of these needs then became the "hook" I used to attract employees. Whatever business you are in, you need to understand the wants of the particular people who are your potential coworkers. I advertise these benefits on flyers, on business cards, or on anything I use to attract people to apply for a job. Remember, people will ask the following question, "Why should I apply for a job with you rather than with Joe Blow down the street? Do you fulfill my wants?" Here is an example of a flyer that focuses on wants.

WE'RE YOUR BEST CHOICE!

HOURS? **WE'LL WORK AROUND YOUR SCHEDULE.**

MONEY? **TALK WITH US.**

FUN? **YOU'LL LIKE THE PEOPLE YOU WORK WITH.**

RAISES? **WE REWARD PERFORMANCE.**
APPLY TODAY!!

When it comes to attracting potential employees, we must be creative. We do this by first knowing who might be interested in our type of work; Secondly, by knowing how to reach them; thirdly, by knowing what their wants are and then appealing to these wants. Think about it for a moment. How do advertisers sell their products? They appeal to what people *want,* not what they need. Obtaining applicants is a sales technique. Successful sales involves thinking about customer *wants* first and *needs* second. What can you give your potential coworkers that meets their wants?

Remember, bait the hook with applicant wants. In today's tight employment market, it is not enough to do our best. We must do what is necessary!

Chapter 1 Summary

- Attracting good people needs to be a #1 priority.

- We need to know the type of people who will be interested and successful in our business.

- We need to know where to find the people we want to hire.

- We need to understand the wants and needs of our potential coworkers.

- We need to advertise the benefits of working for us.

- Filling the applicant pipeline requires a constant, consistent effort.

Chapter 2

Twelve Hiring Tips

Principle: It is easier to hire someone
than it is to fire them!

Have you ever hung wallpaper without using a plumb line? Cooked a new dish without first consulting a recipe? Painted a door or window without first preparing the surface? If so, what did you learn? Benjamin Franklin said, "Haste makes waste." So it is with hiring. If you are merely concerned with hiring a warm body, you will not make the time to properly hire. Proper hiring does take time but often managers are in such a hurry that they neglect this important activity.

If we hurry through the interview, taking very little time to get to know the candidate, or provide very little training, they will attach little importance to their job. I sincerely believe that people are more open to learning at the time of hiring than at any other time. Therefore, the interview and the first two weeks on the job are absolutely critical.

TIP #1- Use a good application form (see example at the end of this chapter). An application form is the basic document in the hiring process, but it is only as good as the questions it asks and the candidate's answers. A good application form should give you the following information:

- Personal information about the candidate- current address, telephone number, and previous home address. This tells you the stability and qualifications of the applicant to work in the U.S.

- Employment interest- when can they work and what special skills do they have that might help them with their job.

- Background information- felonies or misdemeanor convictions, past acts of violence or harassment.

- Education- schools attended, grades, favorite and least favorite classes, extra-curricular activities gives you insight into the applicant's dependability and initiative.

- Personal references (see example at end of chapter)- Use schoolteachers, a doctor, a minister, or a coach. I never ask for friends or family.

- Employment record (see example at end of chapter)- the last three employers with employment history and contact person. Contacting previous employers can be tricky. Many are afraid to say anything negative. There are two essential elements that can affect an employment reference. First, that you properly introduce yourself, and second, that you talk with someone who actually supervised the candidate. I always ask, "Would you hire this person again?" If they will not respond to a telephone call, I ask if I can fax them a reference form.

Here is an example of an introduction for a reference check.

"Hello. My name is _____. I own a business known as _____ and I'm calling in reference to an employment application for _____. He/she states that he/she has worked for you. Could I verify some information with you?"

- Authorization and understanding certification. This is a critical section that is to be signed by the candidate. It gives you the right to contact references and to conduct background checks should you choose to do so. This should be reviewed by a lawyer

TIP #2- During the interview, candidates will tend to exaggerate their strengths and minimize their weaknesses. You therefore must be skilled at reviewing the application and in conducting the interview.

The interview is a critical step in the hiring process. There are at least three purposes for an interview:

- To share information about your business with the candidate, including your values and expectations.

- To receive as much information as possible from the candidate so as to make an intelligent hiring decision.

- To give the candidate an opportunity to clarify and amplify information given on the employment application.

Many people hire by "gut feeling" or "intuition" only to find that these methods are inaccurate and misleading. If you find the prospect of firing an employee distasteful, then you must take the interview process seriously. Interviewing requires skill, but with practice you can become good at it. Remember, it is easier to not hire a person than it is to fire him!

My goal here is to take some of the guesswork out of hiring. The key to hiring is not to dismiss how you feel about a person, but to have some tools to supplement first impressions.

Tip #3- Allow enough time for the interview. I have found that it takes 30-60 minutes to evaluate a candidate.

Tip #4- Use an interview form that reminds you of questions to ask (see example at end of chapter). This will help you keep the interview focused and make it less likely you'll forget to cover some important information. Also, interviews can often deteriorate into idle conversation. A checklist of questions will prevent this from happening. You can prepare the questions in advance and leave room on the form for notes and comments. This will help remind you later as to why you liked or disliked a particular candidate. When you hire a person, the form could be placed in their file. It may come in handy for future reference should a problem arise.

Tip #5- Ask questions that require more than a "yes" or "no" response. For example, note the difference between the following questions: "Do you like working with customers?" "Give me an example of a time when you dealt with an upset customer." Sometimes a question that requires a "yes" or "no" can be used when you are trying to get agreement from the candidate, or when you are determining if it is an appropriate time for closure. For example, "You understand that this is an 8-5 job?" or, "Do you have any other questions?"

Also, ask questions that require candidates to describe the behavior, feelings, and actions that took place in past circumstances that might be similar to circumstances they are likely to encounter in their job with you. For example, if the position you are trying to fill requires good teamwork, you might ask, "Tell me about a time when you had a challenge working with another employee. How did you handle it?"

It is important to remember that the interview should not cause the candidate to feel as if he/she is being "interrogated."

Tip #6- Listen more than you talk. Someone has aptly observed that God gave us two ears and one mouth so we would listen twice as much as we talk!

Effective listening reads between the lines. What the candidate does not say may be as important as what is said. For example, suppose you ask the question, "What situations in your life might cause you to have a problem getting to work on time?" Then candidate responds, ""I've had a few problems with my car." What is the candidate really saying? "My car is not reliable?" "I miss work regularly and use my car as an excuse?" "I am an honest person?" You must figure out what is really being said.

Vague responses may be a red flag because they may be an attempt to conceal or misrepresent information. Therefore, when in doubt, follow up with another question. For example, what question might you follow up with if an applicant said, "Most of my previous employers liked my work"? Here is a possible follow-up question: "Tell me about an employer that you had problems with."

Do not listen only for factual information, but listen for attitudes. Attitudes toward customers, fellow coworkers, and management are often the best indicator of future performance. I vividly remember asking a person what a previous employer would tell me was one of her weaknesses. She replied, "He would tell you that I like to get things done the way I feel they should be done." If I had been alert, I would have followed up with another question.

After hiring her I found out she didn't like to follow directions!

Some candidates may be good, even very good, workers, but poor at responding to interview questions. They may be shy or nervous due to language problems or inexperience with interviews. You must therefore use other screening tools to evaluate them.

Silence can often be an effective listening tool. When you ask a question, do not be afraid to wait for a response. Sometimes when the candidate takes a moment to answer, interviewers jump in and begin talking. Waiting a moment invites honest answers. So, be patient.

Effective listening enables you to ask follow-up questions. Do not be like a robot, just going through the motions.

Tip #7- If you like the candidate, immediately sell the benefits of working for you. The hiring interview is a great time to convince good candidates that they have come to the right place. You need to understand what the individual is looking for in a job and match your position to their wants and needs.

Tip #8- Insure that the interview meets all legal requirements. You, or the person doing the interviewing, are responsible for discrimination-free dealings with all job candidates. Chapter 14 reviews some of these rules and laws. Contact your local labor board or Secretary of State to receive accurate information about the regulations in your area.

Tip #9- Offer conditional employment contingent upon satisfactory results of reference checks. This is especially important if you feel good about the candidate. You don't want to let a good one get away! I also tell the candidate that there will be a two-week trial period so that we both feel good about the arrangement.

Tip #10- Look beyond your gut feeling in making the hiring decision. You must carefully analyze and review all of the information you have collected on the candidates you have interviewed. There are three categories that should help in making this decision:

- The interview.
- Employment reference checks.
- Personal references.

Consider the following guidelines as you weigh this information:

Evaluate the interview in light of all the information you have. Some people may be good interviewees and poor employees. Others may be poor interviewees and good employees.

Prioritize the information you have received. Some people give a higher priority to the interview. Others to the references.

Look for repeated themes in the comments of references. Are there common concerns, or common positive responses relative to reliability, work habits, and honesty? The more uniformity among references the more dependable the information.

While your first impressions of the candidate may ultimately prove correct, don't let your desperate need to hire someone cause you to ignore obvious or even subtle red flags. Here can be seen the value of having more than one candidate to choose from. This is a goal all business owners should be working toward. When you are the busiest is when you usually need the most help!

Sometimes you may want to conduct a second interview with a particular candidate. If the information you receive from references is incomplete or conflicting, a second interview offers you the opportunity to ask additional questions. Remember that hiring the wrong person can often be worse than hiring no one at all!

Tip #11- Clearly communicate your expectations at the time of hiring. Most people come to their new job with little understanding of what is expected of them. I have found that people are the most open to direction and guidance at the time of hiring. Therefore, communicating our expectations at the time of hiring can save hours later on. I use a simple form to communicate this. I call it a "Coworker Understanding of Expectations." See the end of this chapter for an example. I take 10-15 minutes at the time of hire to go over this form sentence by sentence with new coworkers. I give them the opportunity to ask questions to clarify what it is I expect of them. When problems come up later, I go back to our discussion of expectations and reinforce what I shared with them at the time of hiring.

Tip # 12- Develop "Team Rules and a Disciplinary Policy" and give it to the new coworker at the time of hiring. I have had business owners say to me that this is one of the most valuable suggestions they have ever received. It has saved countless problems and headaches for me. A team rules and disciplinary policy accomplishes at least two things:

It lets the coworker know up-front what is acceptable and non-acceptable behavior. Sometimes owners and managers leave their people in the dark relative to honest versus dishonest behavior.

It lets them know exactly what will happen if they fail to follow the rules. The example at the end of this chapter contains two sections. The first section lets employees know what I consider serious violations. The second section indicates the steps that will be taken should they choose not to follow the rules of the job.

I have coworkers sign this form indicating they have read it. Later on when a problem occurs, I take out the form they signed and review it with them.

Hiring is one of the most important activities a business owner or manager will be involved in. Remember, minutes invested up-front can save hours of problems later on!

Chapter 2 Summary

- A few minutes spent up-front in the hiring process can save hours later on.

- A proper interview takes time and skill.

- The decision to hire someone should be arrived at through analysis, rather than gut feeling.

- Expectations should be communicated at the time of hiring.

Sample Employment Application Form

Section 1 – Personal Information

Name (last, first, middle): _____

Present Address (city, state, zip code): _____

_____ **No. years there** _____

Previous Address (city, state, zip code): _____

_____ **No. years there** _____

Social Security Number _____

Home Telephone _____Work Telephone _____

OK to call at work? Y   N

Goals (What would you like to be doing in 2 years?) _____

_____

_____

_____

Section 2 – Employment Interest

Can you work 8 am – 5 pm, Monday through Friday?   Y   N

Starting wage desired $ _____ per _____

List special skills, training, experience which might help you while working for us:

_____

_____

_____

What is the most important to you? Place a 1 by the most important, 2 by the next, and so forth.

___ Benefits
___ Work schedule
___ Adequate income
___ Paid vacation
___ Advancement

Section 3 – Background Information

Have you ever been convicted of a felony offense?   Y   N

Have you ever been convicted of a misdemeanor offense?   Y   N

Have you been convicted of a driving offense?   Y   N

Drivers License # _____ State _____

Expiration _____ Restrictions _____

Have you ever threatened or committed an act of violence, harassment or discrimination against a fellow employee, customer, or any other person?   Y   N

If you answered yes to any of the above, please explain.

_____

_____

Section 4 – Education

School most recently attended _____ Location _____

Last grade completed _____ Grade point average   A   B   C   D

Are you now enrolled in school?   Y   N

If yes, night classes ___ day classes ___

Classes taken that might help you with your work with us?

_____

_____

_____

Section 5 – Employment Record

Do you have another name you have used with previous employers?
Y   N

If yes, what is the name? _____

Company _____
Immediate supervisor _____ Tel. No. _____
Length of employment from _____ to _____
Reason for leaving _____

Company _____
Immediate supervisor _____ Tel. No. _____
Length of employment from _____ to _____
Reason for leaving _____

Company _____
Immediate supervisor _____ Tel. No. _____
Length of employment from _____ to _____
Reason for leaving _____

Section 6 – Personal References

List names, addresses and telephone numbers of 3 people who know you. Do not list relatives.

Name _____
How long they have known you _____
Relationship to you _____
Address _____
_____
Occupation _____ Telephone _____

Name _____
How long they have known you _____
Relationship to you _____
Address _____
_____
Occupation _____ Telephone _____

Name _____
How long they have known you _____
Relationship to you _____
Address _____
_____
Occupation _____   Telephone _____

Section 7 – Agreement
See a competent labor attorney for this section.

PERSONAL REFERENCE CHECKS

Name _____ Date of Contact _____

	#1	#2
Name		
Telephone #		
1. How long and in what capacity have you known the applicant?		
2. What are this person's positive characteristics?		
3. Negative characteristics?		
4. Will this person show up for work?		
5. Are there personal problems that might hinder this person from fulfilling the job?		

EMPLOYMENT REFERENCES

Name _____   Date of Contact _____

	#1	**#2**
Date of Contact		
Contact Person		
Telephone		
Ending Wage		
1. How long and in what capacity did you know the applicant?		
2. What responsibilities did the employee have?		
3. Did you find he/she dependable?		
4. Work on time?		
5. Fulfill job requirements?		
6. Cooperate well with supervisor and other employees?		
7. Why did employee leave?		
8. Would you re-hire?		

9. Has applicant ever been convicted of a crime or driving offense?		
10. Committed an act of violence?		
11. Harassment or discrimination against a customer or employee or other person?		

INTERVIEW FORM

Name _____ Date of Contact _____

Section 1 PERSONAL INFORMATION		Comments
1. First impression of a candidate.	+ Friendly, neat in appearance, on time for interview - Late, unkempt, overly reserved	
2. What situations in your life might cause you to have a problem getting to work on time and fulfilling job requirements?	+ Has no problems - No car, no baby-sitter, may move, etc.	
3. Tell me about your goals. What's most important to you?	+Only wants to support family. Has good family values.	
Section 2 EMPLOYMENT INTEREST		
4. Tell me about how your past experience will help you with working for us?	+Gives specific reasons. -Has little to say about past experiences.	

5. Working for us requires that you work well with a team member and treat customers in a friendly manner. Why do you think you could be successful at this?	+Has had positive experiences working with others. -Has had little experience. Expresses concerns about abilities.	
SECTION 4 EDUCATION		
6. How will your school, family, or work experience assist you with working for us?	+Gives some specific ideas. -Sees no relationship.	
7. Tell me about a time you had to work closely with other people. What did you like most? What did you like least?	+Liked working with others. Tried to get along with others. Was flexible. -Preferred working alone. Didn't like certain people. Never worked closely with others.	
8. Tell me about a time when you had to follow strict procedures or directions.	+Followed directions. Adapted well to changing situations. -Procedures created stress. Didn't enjoy structure.	

9. When I call your previous employer, what will he/she say are your best qualities? Your two greatest weaknesses?	+Was dependable. -Listen very carefully to candidate's answers to weaknesses. Question candidate so you understand. Look for dependability and ability to work with others.	
10.		
11.		

Coworker Understanding
of Expectations

WHAT YOU CAN EXPECT FROM US

We realize that you will probably not make a career out of working with us. However, your employment with us can be of great help to your future. If you will do your part, we can promise you that you will learn the following skills:

1. Customer Service — How to effectively deal with customers
2. Teamwork — How to work effectively with a team of coworkers
3. Leadership — How to take the initiative at a job and become a leader
4. Discipline — How to develop self control, which is critical to success in life

Each of these skills will help you grow and develop, thus preparing you for a secure future. We will provide the opportunities, but it is up to you.

WHAT WE EXPECT FROM YOU
Customer Service
You agree to provide excellent customer service so that our customers:

1. Feel welcome when they first enter or telephone our place of business.
2. Feel that we care about them as individuals.
3. Feel that we appreciate their business.
4. Feel that we care about the quality of our product.
5. Feel that we care when they have a complaint.

Teamwork
You agree to be a team player so that other team members:
  1. Can count on you.
  2. Can trust you.
  3. Enjoy working with you.

Responsibility
You agree to be a responsible coworker so that your owner and manager:
  1. Can trust you.
  2. Feel you care about the store and your job.

You understand that true service is helping customers feel good about themselves. You fully understand what your owner/manager expects of you.

Coworker Signature _____
Date _____
Manager Signature _____
Date _____
First Evaluation _____
Date Goal _____

Team Rules and Disciplinary Policy

PURPOSE: Our business will be as successful as the team we have hired. You are an important member of our team. For our team to be successful we need rules to guide what we do. These rules will help you work with other team members and will let you know up front what we expect of you. Violations of team rules affect everyone. This policy will explain team rules and the results you can expect when a rule is broken.

TEAM RULE VIOLATIONS

There are two types:

1. Grounds for immediate termination
- Stealing or mishandling of money
- Using drugs or alcohol while working
- Giving away products or merchandise
- Refusing to follow a direct order from the manager or supervisor
- Assault of a team member or customer
- Being rude to customers

2. Serious Violations
Failing to:
- Greet, talk with, and thank our customers
- Answer the telephone in a friendly manner
- Suggest other products to our customers
- Handle customer complaints in a friendly, sensitive manner
- Stay busy at all times so that other coworkers do not have to do your work
- Get along with other team members - no backbiting, gossiping, putting down
- Failing to be at work on time every shift
- Follow approved opening and closing procedures
- Failing to keep the workplace clean

Acts of Commission:
- Bringing friends into the work area
- Receiving or making personal calls except in an emergency

Should one of these team rules be violated, the following steps will occur until the behavior is either corrected or the coworker terminated:

- First - You will be reminded as to the proper behavior.
- Second - You will have a sit-down, face-to-face talk with your manager.
- Third - You will sign a written warning form that will be placed in your file.
- Fourth - Your work hours will be reduced.
- Fifth - You will be terminated.

I have read "Team Rules and Disciplinary Policy" and understand the rules and what will happen should I violate the rules.

Coworker_____

Date _____

SECTION 2

MOTIVATING AND

RETAINING COWORKERS

Chapter 3

Why do People do What They do?

Principle: Coworkers seek to satisfy universal needs in different ways.

In the movie "My Fair Lady," Henry Higgins exclaims, "Why can't a woman be more like a man? Some managers ask, "Why can't my coworkers be more like me?" They learn sooner or later that people are different. This is the great lesson leaders have learned. However, some managers are so self-centered they simply can't understand why people don't see things their way. For these managers it's "my way or the highway!"

Leaders know that people are different from each other. They seek to understand their coworkers individually so that they can assist them to grow and to be successful in their job.

The first step in this learning process is to be aware of the basic universal needs of people and the truth that coworkers will seek to satisfy these universal needs in different ways. The second step is to become acquainted with each coworker in order to understand what is important to them.

Four Universal Needs

Personality and motivation are extremely complex issues; hence the myriad of books on personality types and motivational theory. I have found that people do what they do to satisfy a need or want. This could be diagrammed as follows:

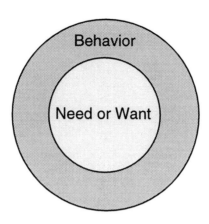

For example, physical needs are extremely important. If people are hungry they will do almost anything to get food. Jean Valjean, in Victor Hugo's *Les Miserables*, risked his life to obtain a loaf of bread.

Managers need to understand what the universal needs and wants of people are in order to better understand why coworkers do what they do.

Senator Robert F. Bennett in *Gaining Control* suggests that all behavior can be traced to four common needs: 1) the need for life; 2) the need for self-esteem; 3) the need for belonging; and, 4) the need for fun and variety.

He compares these needs to a wheel.

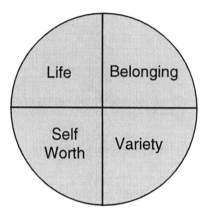

When all of these needs are being satisfactorily met, life "rolls along" smoothly. When one need is not being satisfied, that area becomes "flat" and our life is not smooth. For example, if life or physical needs are not being met our life looks like this:

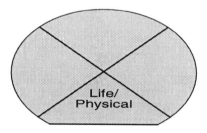

Let's examine each of these four needs and how an understanding of them can assist us in dealing with our coworkers.

Life/Physical Needs

Perhaps you remember from a college or university class Maslow's *Hierarchy of Needs*. He placed the physical needs at the very base of his pyramid and stated that if this need is "flat" an individual will neglect all other needs to satisfy this one. Nourishment, rest, clothing, shelter, and safety are elements of this need; it is particularly important to people who must support and sustain themselves. For them, money is the means to satisfy this need. Should they not make enough money to meet their physical needs, they will look for a job that does. When people make enough to meet this need, they tend to focus on meeting other needs.

Those who hire young people who are being supported by their parents need to realize that money might not be a motivating need for them. They might be working for party or gas money or merely because they like working with other people.

The Need for Self-Worth

At the core of our being is this powerful thing called self-worth. Self-worth is how one feels about himself or herself and is influenced to a great degree by how others treat us. Studies show that the way a child is raised has a profound influence on the child's feelings of self-worth.

Dorothy L. Nolte has captured this idea in the following:

CHILDREN LEARN WHAT THEY LIVE

If a child lives with criticism, he learns to condemn.

If a child lives with hostility, he learns to fight.

If a child lives with fear, he learns to be apprehensive.

If a child lives with pity, he learns to feel sorry for himself.

If a child lives with jealousy, he learns to hate.

If a child lives with encouragement, he learns to be confident.

If a child lives with tolerance, he learns to be patient.

If a child lives with praise, he learns to be appreciative.

If a child lives with acceptance, he learns to love.

If a child lives with approval, he learns to like himself.

If a child lives with recognition, he learns to have a goal.

If a child lives with fairness, he learns justice.

If a child lives with security, he learns to have faith in himself and in those about him.

If a child lives with honesty, he learns what truth is.

If a child lives with friendliness, he learns that the world is a nice place in which to live.

As managers, we need to realize that many people have impacted the lives of those we choose to hire. Our coworkers might be compared to an artist's canvas, whereon many people have left their impressions. By the time we hire them, their feelings of self-worth have been basically formed.

What are the differences between people with a high self-worth and those with low self-worth?

High/Positive Self-worth	Low/Negative Self-worth
Self-confident	Timid
Positive and optimistic	Negative and pessimistic
Outgoing/friendly	Shy/anti-social

Managers and supervisors either build or tear down self-worth. Often we are not aware of how we impact other people. This impact can be illustrated as follows. A coworker's self-worth might be compared to a balloon. Each person we hire has a self-worth that is inflated to a different degree. What we do either inflates or deflates their self-worth. Negative, critical behavior is like a sharp pin that deflates them. A positive atmosphere on the other hand inflates self-worth. Coworkers and customers also affect their self-worth. An unresolved dispute with a coworker can poison the workplace. An angry, abusive customer can deflate some coworkers for days.

What is the value to us as managers of creating a positive work environment? Ken Blanchard, author of <u>One Minute Manager</u>, says, "People who feel good about themselves produce good results."

The Need for Love/Belonging

Most people have a social need, that is, a desire to interact with other people. Thus we see the popularity of athletic teams, clubs, and other social groups. Personal relationships are very important to us.

People have this need to a greater or lesser degree. Some prefer to be "loners," possibly as a result of past experience and/or low self-worth. These coworkers will usually be more successful in jobs that require little social interaction.

Coworkers who feel part of a team, who "connect" with other coworkers, are usually happier on the job and more motivated. Our assignment, then, is to help create a cooperative smooth-running team. This can only be accomplished by a leader who sees the importance of developing people.

The Need for Variety/Fun

One of the great challenges business owners and managers face today is "burnout." Not only do we face "burnout," but our coworkers do also. When people do the same things for an extended period of time, they become bored. Boredom leads not only to a lack of enthusiasm and motivation but also to less productivity. Most managers are insensitive to this need and plod along ,wondering why coworkers are not more enthusiastic about their job. Leaders understand this important need, and are constantly trying to create variety and fun in the workplace.

These four needs-- life/physical needs; self-worth; belonging; and the need for variety/fun are what motivate our coworkers. The need they focus on today may not be tomorrow's need. This is where problems come from. John Maxwell reported a survey by the Barna Research Group of over twelve hundred people. The participants were asked to identify their single most serious need or problem. Here are the results:

39%	Financial
16%	Job-Related
12%	Personal Health
8%	Time and Stress
7%	Parenting
6%	Educational Attainment
3%	Fear of Crime
3%	Personal Relationships

Compare this list with the four needs we have been talking about. Do you see how all relate to one of the four, with the top three dealing with physical/life needs?

Finding out how coworkers seek to satisfy their needs

People seek to satisfy these four universal needs in different ways. Leaders, therefore, get to know their coworkers so they can discover what I call their "hot buttons." Hot buttons are ways they seek to fulfill their needs. For example, not all people seek to satisfy their need for self-worth in the same ways. Some do it through money and position, while others increase self-worth through goal setting and achievement. Some people like public recognition while others hate it. One manager tried to motivate his coworkers by asking, "Isn't it important to you that we are #1?" For some it was important, for others it was not. Another manager couldn't understand why his youthful coworkers were not motivated to win tickets to the opera!

The following diagram illustrates the four universal needs of people and suggests different ways coworkers try to satisfy these needs. We can assume that the most basic need our workers have is economic. They will not usually stay with a job that does not satisfy this need.

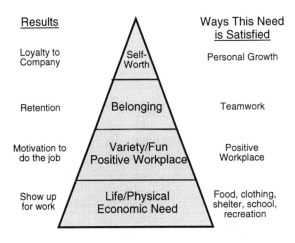

Leaders understand that to create coworker motivation they must go beyond the economic need. Leaders understand that to get loyalty they must do what others are not willing to do.

How do we know what motivates our coworkers?

- Ask them what is most meaningful to them: money, teamwork, or recognition?
- Watch coworkers and observe what seems to be their "hot buttons."
- Maintain on-going communication by asking questions and listening to their feelings and viewpoints.
- Conduct periodic interviews to find out how they are doing. Some leaders call this a retention interview. They seek to find out how coworkers are feeling about their job and life in general.

Leaders constantly try to be in tune with their coworkers and they seek to establish a workplace that meets these four needs. They are prepared to give their coworkers assistance. The following chapters will focus on how leaders do this.

Chapter 3 Summary

- People are motivated when their wants and needs are satisfied.

- People have four basic needs: physical/life needs, belonging, self-worth, and variety or fun.

- People will try and satisfy their wants and needs in different ways.

- Leaders try to understand what motivates each of their coworkers.

Chapter 4

The Secret to Coworker Motivation and Retention

Principle: Internal motivation is more productive and lasting than external motivation.

Everywhere I go I hear managers say things like this, "Why can't my employees take initiative?" "How do I get people to follow the guidelines?" "Why aren't my employees more motivated?"

Motivation! What is this mysterious attribute that almost every manager wishes his or her employees had? To me, motivation is the physical, mental, and emotional energy we bring to a task. But I have found that motivation doesn't come automatically with a paycheck. While money is important, the key to motivation and retention is *leadership* on the part of business owners and managers.

There are two types of motivation, external and internal. External is imposed upon us by some other person or need. We are motivated to do something because we feel we *have* to.   This type of motivation is usually based on fear, obligation, or a strong need to survive. Fear causes the coworker to feel, "If I don't do this, I'll lose my job." Obligation causes the coworker to think, "I want to do a good job so my manager will respect me." And the need to survive can be expressed thusly: "I have to be able to pay my bills."   External motivation is often what keeps employees doing their job on a day-to-day basis, but not always doing it well.

Internal motivation comes from within because we *want* to do what is asked. It is the key to retention. People can usually get another job and earn the money they need. But they stay with a job because of internal motivation. This type of motivation is based on job satisfaction.   The coworker enjoys working with his manager, other coworkers, and enjoys the job. Leaders are able to establish a positive, pleasant atmosphere in their place of business. When this is created, coworkers enjoy their job more. The following diagram illustrates these two types of motivation:

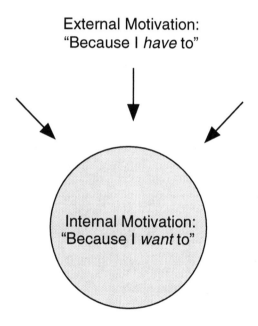

There are three types of management styles that draw on either external or internal motivation.

The Drill Sergeant

We've all seen the Drill Sergeant in action either because we've served in the military or watched movies in which this character appears. Drill Sergeants are masters at external motivation. Their major managerial tool is a cattle prod. They are very insensitive to the thoughts, feelings, and concerns of their coworkers. They deflate their coworker's self worth. Their management style is characterized by threats, put downs, sarcasm, and order giving. Those who work for this manager are certainly motivated to do their job! However, their motivation is out of fear – fear of the wrath of the manager. They work hard while their manager is physically present, but as soon as he or she is gone, all hell breaks out. People build strong resentments toward the Drill Sergeant and the moment they are able to find another job they say, " Take this job and shove it." The consequences of fear are grudges, resentment, and the desire to get even.

The problem with the Drill Sergeant is that coworkers are not self-motivated. They are motivated by outward pressure and as soon as that pressure is removed they quit doing what is expected.

The Buddy-Buddy

These managers believe that chumminess and accommodation are the keys to motivating people. They think, "If my coworkers think I like them, and if I am agreeable and laid-back, they will work hard and be responsible." The management style of the Buddy-Buddy is therefore one of undue leniency, familiarity, and often favoritism. They have problems giving needed directions, applying company rules, and reporting misconduct. They make deals, concede, and compromise. What the buddy-buddy doesn't realize is that this management style is damaging to morale because by removing discipline people can't trust them. For example, parents who try to be a Buddy-Buddy with their children undermine their sense of security by allowing them to do whatever they want. Coworkers, like children, need boundaries and a sense of discipline. The Buddy-Buddy just isn't aware of this. And you and I know that people will take advantage of this type of manager. The motivation to do things because of mere duty or friendship is never strong enough to build loyalty.

Of the two management styles discussed so far, which one do you think is the most damaging to coworker motivation? At first glance you might answer, "the Drill Sergeant." Drill Sergeants create immediate harm, but the Buddy-Buddy's style, which seems to be the most innocent, may in the long run create the greatest harm! Why? Because the effects may not be noticed until there are big problems.

In my seminars I ask all of the Drill Sergeants to raise their hands. In a group of 50, maybe only about two will admit to being Drill Sergeants. And when they do, some of the group will usually make fun of them. When I ask the Buddy-Buddies to raise their hands, about twenty will admit it. No one usually says anything negative about them, and yet, they may be the most dangerous kind of manager. Why are more people the Buddy-Buddy type of manager? Possibly because it takes a certain personality type to be a Drill Sergeant while it is easier for people to slip into the

Buddy-Buddy style in their anxiety to be liked and not to make waves.

The Leader

While the Drill Sergeant motivates out of fear, and the Buddy-Buddy out of chumminess and leniency, the Leader focuses on cooperation through the development of coworkers. Neither the Drill Sergeant nor the Buddy-Buddy understands the importance of people development because each is motivated by an overwhelming self-interest—the Drill Sergeant to be obeyed; the Buddy-Buddy to be liked. The Leader understands that his number one role is to develop his coworkers.

The Leader also understands the difference between being liked and being respected. Most managers want to be liked and respected. For example, Drill Sergeants are usually not liked and probably don't care! But they do want to be respected and often are. On the other hand the Buddy-Buddy is probably liked, but is usually not respected. The Leader is both liked and respected, a combination essential to motivation and to retention. When a manager is respected, coworkers work hard. Respect is based on three qualities: fairness with people, honesty, and competency. When a manager is liked, coworkers are loyal to their job. Leaders are liked because they first like their employees. They do this because they sincerely <u>care</u> about their employees. They care because they genuinely like people and know that the success of their business is, to a great degree, in the hands of their coworkers. They, therefore, make the time to develop their people.   Drill Sergeants are not concerned about the development of their people. They are concerned with results and results are obtained through intimidation. Buddy-Buddies care, but in an unrealistic manner. They hope that by showing concern and "sensitivity" they will motivate team members to do their best. The Leader cares to such a degree that he requires a great deal of his coworkers and focuses time and energy to develop them.

C.A.R.E.S.

I have identified five key characteristics of Leaders that cause employees to not only respect them but to like them. These characteristics are represented in the acronym CARES.

Communicates effectively

Acts with vision

Recognizes contributions

Earns trust

Strengthens team members

These five qualities assist the Leader in meeting the needs of his/her coworkers. Each of the following chapters will review one of these five important qualities of a leader.

Chapter 4 Summary

- Motivation is both external and internal.

- When internally motivated, people do things because they <u>want</u> to.

- Three types of leadership are: a) The Drill Sergeant; b) The Buddy-Buddy, c) The Leader.

- Leaders tap into the internal motivation of their coworkers.

- An effective leader <u>cares</u> about his/her coworkers.

Chapter 5

Communicate Effectively

A

R

E

S

*Principle: The Leader establishes an atmosphere of
effective communication by sharing important
information and by listening to coworkers.*

Communication is the on-going flow of information
between manager and coworker. It is to the workplace

what the arteries and veins are to the physical body. The blockage of arteries and veins can lead to death!

Someone once said the following and I absolutely believe it, "You cannot *not* communicate!" Whether we say something or not we are communicating. We are communicating our ideas, our confidence, our negativity, and our interest or indifference. An effective manager realizes that ongoing positive communication with coworkers is essential. I am convinced that 90% of the problems managers encounter could be eliminated with effective communication. The following diagrams illustrate how a Drill Sergeant, Buddy-Buddy, and Leader communicate.

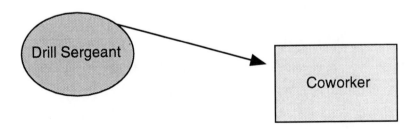

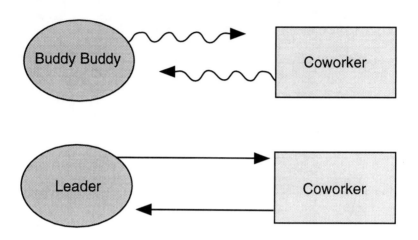

To facilitate communication, a manager needs to be effective at sharing and receiving information. Let's look first at the sharing of information.

Sharing information

This involves two things: first, *what* information a manager gives and, second, *how* the information is given.

It is essential that managers communicate information with their coworkers. When we do this, our coworkers feel that they are a part of the team. It helps them take ownership in the business and its success. I worked for a company where the owners rarely shared information with us. I never felt that I was a part of the team and neither did my coworkers. I have found three important areas that are critical to effective communication on the part of managers.

Setting Priorities

I have asked many people what they thought were the major priorities of their job. I have then asked their managers what they felt the major priorities were. You guessed it! In most cases both the coworker and the manager had different perceptions of job priorities. Here is a prime example of poor communication. The Leader understands that people need to know clearly what the major responsibilities of their job are. The way to accomplish this is to make up a list of what you expect each of your coworkers to do, then prioritize the list by placing a "1" next to what you consider to be the most important activity, a "2" by the second and so on. Finally, sit down with new coworkers and go over this prioritized job description. Here is an example of a job description a manager of a fast food restaurant gives to his people.

- Serve a quality product.
- Treat each customer in a friendly manner.
- Sell other products to our customers.
- Keep the restaurant clean.
- Answer the telephone and take orders in a friendly way.

The Chain of Command

A business consultant found out that when he asked people, "Who is your boss?" many were not quite sure. Coworkers need to know from the beginning whom they report to and from whom they take orders. This is critically important when the owner or manager is not physically present in the business. Knowing "Who's in charge" is important. The Leader understands this and has a clear chain of command for each work shift. The Leader is also supportive of those to whom he has given responsibility and is careful not to step in and do their job. Should the manager step in and handle the matter, it undermines the self-esteem and motivation of the one who had the responsibility in the first place. This is very important in a growing business where an owner or manager must delegate responsibility. Some people have a difficult time giving away authority and therefore constantly step in and run things. This undermines the respect and confidence people have in those to whom they report to.

Updates and Important Information

Most people feel respected and valued when they are kept up to date on the progress and challenges facing the business. Other information, such as achievements and accomplishments of coworkers, is also important. Some managers have a white board which they use to communicate information. They put birthdays on it as well as positive customer comments. They also share reminders about certain things they want coworkers to focus on.

Some managers hold regular team meetings where they get coworkers together for an hour and share information. During these meetings they have a short training presentation. They also recognize outstanding coworker performance and talk about upcoming promotions and advertisements.

Other managers have a weekly or monthly newsletter that updates coworkers on special promotions, activities, and training information. In general, any method the manager can use to communicate information on a regular basis is valuable.

The second ingredient relative to giving information is *how* it is given.

The **way** a manager communicates will determine to a great degree how people respond. I have observed three ways managers communicate with their coworkers: down, across, and up. "Down" is the style of the Drill Sergeant. He communicates in such a way that his people feel they are unimportant and that he/she is "The Boss!" Using intimidation and criticism to get results, he couldn't care less what effect he has on his coworkers. His manner of communication says, "I am up here and you're down there and don't you forget it!"

The Buddy-Buddy communicates "up". Hungry for approval, he wants his coworkers to consider themselves not just as his equals but maybe even his superior. He says, "I'm down here and you're up there."

The Leader communicates "across" by showing respect and concern for her coworkers. She says, "My employees are my #1 asset. We are in this together and I care about them and their success."

There are two essential elements that determine whether we communicate up, down or across. The first is the *words* we use and the second is the *way* we say them. Let's compare the Drill Sergeant, Buddy-Buddy, and the Leader as communicators.

The Words We Use

Most people are unaware of the way they communicate. However, the Drill Sergeant probably understands the way he communicates but doesn't care. He uses words as a whip or a weapon and his words show his negative attitude toward people. These words range from mild to abusive. "Stupid, dumb, ignorant" are the mild ones. Vulgarity, ethnic slurs, and sexual innuendoes are the more serious. Drill Sergeants love sarcasm and say such things as "Do I have to get someone I can count on to do this?" Or, "What have you been doing all day? This place is a mess!" Words that communicate down are usually negative and cause people to feel unimportant and worthless. That's why they're called "put-downs."

The Buddy-Buddy chooses words that ingratiate himself to his coworkers. Because he wants them to feel they are on the same level, he says things like, "Don't worry about it. I'll take care of it." "I won't say anything." "The boss doesn't need to know." The last thing a Buddy-Buddy wants is to hurt his coworkers' feelings. For this reason, he is careful to avoid the "put-downs" of a Drill Sergeant.

The Leader is careful in the choice of his words and understands that words mean different things to different people. He knows the power of words and understands the principle that we communicate up, down, or across. He wants to be respectful of his employees and to show them that he cares, but is not subservient.

How is this done? First, the Leader is courteous and polite to his coworkers. He remembers to thank them for the extra things they do. Even when he disciplines, he is careful about the words he chooses. Second, the Leader uses words that build a positive atmosphere. He avoids negative words that are so common in the workplace today. Instead he uses the language of cooperation. "Let's work together." "We're in this together." "I'm here to help." And third, he is even-tempered and good-humored. Humor in the workplace is like oil in an automobile engine. It reduces friction.

The Leader is also aware that some people do not receive verbal communications well. He understands that written communications are often helpful for some people. I had a coworker who had difficulty following oral instructions. When I wrote the tasks down, they were always completed. Be alert, however, as to whether your coworkers can read English. It's not surprising today to find high school graduates who can't read well. How could this affect your business? Any task that requires the reading of instructions could be a problem.

How we say it

How we say something can be even more powerful than *what* we say. While information is being exchanged through words, there is another conversation going on. It is an exchange of attitude as to how we feel about each other. Our attitude is communicated by voice tone and by body language. This unspoken conversation may communicate more than what is being said. The Drill Sergeant communicates through tone and manner an attitude of disrespect. The Buddy-Buddy communicates a pathetic desire to be accepted and liked. She does not maintain a professional relationship because she is overly familiar.

You have experienced this underlying conversation with managers you have had. For example, in most businesses there is a hierarchical relationship between coworker and boss. We relate according to job position. This is why most coworkers expect their boss to give them direction and even correction. But this does not give the boss permission to treat you in a degrading manner. So, there is a professional and personal relationship between manager and coworker. The Leader shows good balance between the two. He maintains a professional relationship while respecting the personal feelings of his coworkers.

I knew a manager who could tell his employees to go to hell and because of the way he said it, they loved going there! Most of us need to be more sensitive to the way we say things. Voice inflection and body language communicate more than the words we use. Drill Sergeants are masters at putting people down through voice tone and gestures. You can probably picture a Drill Sergeant pointing his finger, scowling, and chewing out a coworker in a rough, condescending tone. How do you picture the Buddy-Buddies? Friendly voice inflection? A smile? A kind look in their eyes?

Leaders are sensitive, yet are careful not to cross over the line by maintaining a professional relationship.

Leaders are skilled at receiving information

Let's look now at receiving information. Managers need to be skilled at understanding their coworker's feelings. Too often, people assume they understand what others are thinking and feeling. Or they assume that others have understood what they have tried to communicate. This leads to countless communication problems.

I have asked hundreds of people what the most important quality was that draws them to another person they admire and respect. The #1 response has been "they like me." When I ask, "how do you know they like you?" The response is usually, "They listen to me." Everyone likes a good listener. Why? It communicates we care. At the heart of listening is *wanting* to hear what another person is saying and feeling. Dale Carnegie put it this way, "You can make more friends in two weeks by becoming a good listener than you can in two years trying to get people interested in you." When you listen to and value the opinions of your coworkers, they have a greater reason for liking you and remaining loyal to you. Effective listening also ensures that we are not just assuming we understand what coworkers understand and feel. Here are four things I have learned about listening to my coworkers.

Listening requires an investment of time

Some managers are task oriented. This means they place a higher value on getting things done than they do on relationships. They do not feel that taking time for communication is important. Yet, if they understood what it means to another person when they listen, they would certainly make the time. A small investment of time to listen can pay big dividends in the motivation and retention of employees.

Listening requires concentration

To understand others, we must concentrate on what they are saying and what they are *not* saying. This means watching body language and listening for what is behind what is being said. Peter Drucker emphasized this when he said, "The most important thing in communication is to hear what isn't said." I look and listen for voice inflection and watch for eye movement and facial expression. I listen during pauses or gaps in the flow of talk, for even silence can mean something—uncertainty, avoidance, or fear.

Listening requires a response

Communication is a two-way street and is facilitated when questions are asked that focus on what the employee has said. This accomplishes two things. First, it lets a person know we are listening; and, second, it gives us information to help us more clearly understand what the person is feeling.

Listening requires that we check for understanding

We need to check to make sure we understand what the other person has said and that he or she understands what we have said. We do this by reflecting or rephrasing what we heard the coworker say or having the coworker repeat what he/she heard us say. Let me illustrate. One of our managers came to work visibly upset. I took her aside and said, "You seem to be upset. Can I help?" She responded by saying she was unhappy with her job. I thought that maybe I was working her too hard, but asked, "What seems to be the problem?" She then told me that one of our coworkers was giving her fits. She described him as rude and irresponsible. I reflected back what I heard her say, "You mean he's not carrying his share. Is that the problem?" She said "No. I mean he never listens to what I say and yesterday he let me know that just because I was the boss didn't mean he had to do what I said!"

We then were able to focus on how she might deal with this person. Since that experience, I have often thought about what might have happened if I had been too busy to communicate with her. What could have happened if I had treated her problem with indifference or had assumed the issue was simply an unequal workload as I first supposed? I could have lost an excellent manager.

Another way Leaders receive information is by soliciting feedback from coworkers. Leaders are constantly asking the question, "What can we do better?" They sincerely want to know how their coworkers see things. Often coworkers in a business see the reality of what is happening that might be missed by management. I remember asking one of my coworkers what we could do better. She responded, "The restaurant isn't appealing to customers. We need to change the décor." Her observation was right on the money and that suggestion helped our business.

Managers who are Leaders are sensitive to whether they communicate up, down, or across. Leaders are in the business of developing people. They let their people know through <u>what</u> they say, <u>how</u> they say it, and their desire to listen that they are on the same team.

Chapter 5 Summary

• Communication is an exchange of information between manager and coworker.

• Leaders let their coworkers know what's going on in the business.

• It is as important <u>how</u> a Leader communicates as <u>what</u> he/she communicates.

• Careful listening is as essential as clear speaking.

Chapter 6

C

Act with vision and purpose

R

E

S

Principle: Leaders help coworkers
set and achieve goals.

There's an old Texas saying, "You can't light a fire with a wet match." So it is with managing people. If you want them to be enthusiastic, then you need to be enthusiastic. I'm not talking about a phony enthusiasm. We must believe in what we are saying. Negative, pessimistic people are simply not fun to be around. Leaders who have inspired me have had a passion for what they were doing. Their passion ignited a desire within me to do my best. But how do you ignite your own enthusiasm, your own passion for your business, and how do you communicate that to your coworkers? Here are four steps you might consider.

Step 1- Catch the vision yourself

I have talked with many business owners and managers who tell me they are "burned out." How does this happen? When what we are doing lacks meaning and purpose, we soon get tired of it. Most people who have taken college or university classes have felt at times, "What relevance does this class have to my life!" The way to spark or rekindle the fire is to attach meaning and purpose to what we are doing.

Three workers were carrying bricks from a truck and placing them in a pile at a construction site. When asked what they were doing, one said, "I'm carrying bricks." The second said, "I'm making a wall." The third said, "I'm building a cathedral."

Who can get excited about carrying bricks or building a wall? What was the difference between these three workers? Only the third had the big picture. This gave him a motivating purpose and made him feel a part of something important.

Leaders who effectively supervise their coworkers do so because they have "super vision." They have a strong sense of purpose. They want to make a difference in peoples' lives and they understand how their business is of benefit to people. You might say they have a dream.

You can't expect your coworkers to catch a vision you don't have. There is a well-known proverb, "Without vision, the people perish."

How do you catch such a vision that inspires and motivates others? Ask yourself this question, "What service does my business provide that is important to people?" Once you know this, you have discovered a key to not only motivating yourself, but your coworkers. For example, a company that places temporary workers determined they were in the business of solving people problems. They solved the problem of workers who need a job and they solved the problem of businesses getting workers. Ray Kroc, the founder of McDonald's, knew what business he was in. He said, "I'm not selling hamburgers, I'm selling dreams." What was the dream he was selling? The dream of business ownership.

Step 2- Determine a goal for your business

In Lewis Carroll's, <u>Alice in Wonderland,</u> the Cheshire cat offers Alice some advice that is relevant to business owners and managers:

"Cheshire Puss, would you tell me, please, which way I ought to walk from here?" "That depends a good deal on where you want to get to," said the Cat. "I don't much care where---"said Alice. "Then it doesn't matter which way you walk," said the Cat. "---so long as I get <u>somewhere</u>," Alice added as an explanation. "Oh, you're sure to do that," said the Cat, "if only you walk long enough."

Understanding the service you provide to customers is only half of the formula. You need to have a personal goal for your business and for your coworkers. This could be a monetary goal. It could mean becoming #1 in your industry or having the best customer service in your community.

One of the people I admire is Fred Deluca, the co-founder of Subway Sandwiches. Fred has had a dream and a goal that has kept him ignited and on fire. That dream has been to provide his team of franchise owners with the tools and knowledge to become the number one fast food chain in every market they enter. He has transmitted this goal to his coworkers and they have been enthusiastic about pursuing it.

You will find that when you know what you want to accomplish, then you are most effective as a manager. You have a purpose, a goal. You are usually the least effective when you lack purpose and meaning in what you are doing. This is when the business loses its fun.

You might consider putting steps 1 and 2 on a card and placing it where you can see the card every day.

Step 3- Help coworkers catch the vision

On the wall in a church in England is a sign that reads: "A vision without a task is but a dream. A task without a vision is drudgery. A vision with a task is the hope of the world."

Often business owners ask coworkers to do things without ever telling them *why* they are important, without giving them a vision. Coworkers then see their tasks as mundane, having little importance. It's like carrying bricks. Therefore, a manager must attach importance and meaning to the job. A good question to consider is: "In what ways does this job provide my coworkers with more than just money?"

You can also assist your coworkers to attach meaning to the assigned tasks they are given. Once you have determined the purpose or goal for your business, you can relate each coworker task to that purpose. Take, for example, a business that is based on excellent customer service. Customer service becomes the purpose around which all coworker tasks revolve. The following diagram illustrates this:

Notice in the following two examples how one manager attaches meaning to the job while the other merely assigns tasks.

Manager A	Manager B
Wash your hands after using the bathroom	Wash your hands. It says to our customers we care about their health
Keep the floors clean.	Keep the floors clean. Customers appreciate it
Always thank people for their business	Saying thank you to a customer lets them know we appreciate their business

Step 4- Set meaningful goals with coworkers.

Setting and achieving goals is a powerful way to increase self worth. It also encourages coworkers to feel a part of a business and assists them in taking ownership for what happens. Goals also force people to move out of their comfort zones, thus helping them accomplish more than they normally would. They may also create a healthy and productive competition. Here are eight keys that unlock the power of not just goal setting, but "goal getting."

Key #1- Goals can be set on a team or on an individual basis. Team goals usually relate to the overall success of the business and put the responsibility for accomplishment on the entire team. This can be a very effective way to motivate coworkers to work together and to encourage and help each other.

Individual goals focus on the growth of the individual and are set between the manager and the coworker. This gives the manager a chance to focus on skills she wants the coworker to acquire.

Key #2- Let coworkers help shape the goals. The president of a company I worked for tried to inspire his coworkers by dictating every so often a goal he had come up with. He couldn't understand why very few in the company became excited with his goals. And that was the problem! They were <u>his</u> goals! Self-worth and a sense of belonging are encouraged when we have coworkers involved in the setting of goals. Goals then become "ours" not "yours." Involvement leads to excitement and ownership of a goal and takes advantage of your coworkers' experience and creativity.

Key #3- The reward for accomplishing a goal must be meaningful to the coworker. Usually a monetary goal is motivating but this may not be so with every coworker. You need to determine what is meaningful to your people. Recognition of the accomplishment of a goal is essential.

Key #4- Goals need to be realistic or attainable. The purpose of a goal is to encourage coworkers to stretch, but not to stretch to the point where they snap! Failure to achieve a goal usually leads to discouragement and an unwillingness to set future goals. How do you determine if a goal is reachable? Look at past performance. What have people been able to accomplish in the past? Then set goals that either meet or exceed to a small degree what has been done. People must have faith they can accomplish the goal.

Key #5- The goal must be specific. It has been said that when we deal in generalities we rarely succeed; when we deal with specifics we rarely fail. Note the difference in the following goals: "Increase store volume," and "Increase store volume to $15,000 per week." It is very difficult to focus on a goal that is too general.

Key #6- Goals need to have a deadline. A goal without a deadline is merely a wish. For some businesses, yearly goals are the best. For others, like those that hire entry-level workers, goals are best set on a monthly or even weekly basis. A deadline gives a sense of urgency to the accomplishment of a goal.

Key #7- Goals need to be broken down into "bite sized" pieces. You have probably heard the question, "How do you eat an elephant?" And the response, "One bite at a time!" Breaking a yearly goal down into monthly goals, or a monthly goal into weekly or daily goals is very motivating to people. Often people become discouraged with long range goals and give up along the way.

Key #8- Goals need to be visual. Often goals are written down and placed in a file or a drawer only to be forgotten. Individual goals should be placed where the coworker can see them regularly. Team goals can be displayed where all can see. The United Way has used the power of visual goals very effectively. Have you seen a United Way thermometer with increments starting at the bottom and the goal at the top? As progress is made, the increments are colored in, showing people their progress towards the goal. Managers can use graphs or charts to show the goal and how the team is progressing towards it. This visual reminder keeps coworkers focused on the goal.

Leaders are able to create a motivating work environment by attaching meaning to what their coworkers do and by setting goals with them.

Chapter 6 Summary

* Leaders have a vision and a purpose for what they are doing.

* When coworkers know <u>why</u> they are to do something, they are more likely to be motivated to do it.

* Team and individual goals are a powerful way to motivate people.

* Involve coworkers in the goal setting process.

Chapter 7

C

A

Recognize Contributions

E

S

Principle: Recognizing and rewarding coworkers for contributions is as important as financial remuneration.

You are probably aware of surveys that have been taken of workers and what they like or dislike about their jobs. One survey indicated that the #1 thing they wanted most was to know what was happening in the business. Another survey said that the #1 cause of dissatisfaction among workers was the failure of their supervisors to give them credit and show them appreciation.

My experience both as a coworker and as a manager has shown me that recognition is important to people. There are at least three ways we communicate our satisfaction or dissatisfaction to our coworkers. The first is to praise them, the second is to criticize them, and the third is to not say anything. Which of these three have you found to be the most "demotivating?" To me it's to say nothing. I have noticed that sometimes people prefer negative feedback to no feedback at all. This is evident with children who act up so at least their parents will notice them.

Our coworkers want to be noticed. Each has this important thing called "self-worth." Self worth is defined as how I feel about myself.

Have you noticed that when people feel good about themselves they are more motivated to work and perform well? However, when they are discouraged and feeling down, motivation is low.

Aubrey Daniels in his book, Bringing Out the Best in People, writes, "People do what they do because of what happens to them when they do it." He has found that the one thing managers can do that most influences coworker's behavior is positive reinforcement. Some examples of positive reinforcement are:

- Verbal praise
- Verbal thank you
- Note of appreciation
- A reward such as a day off with pay
- A plaque or gift certificate

Programs like the Boy and Girl Scouts are based on the idea that people want to be recognized, even if it is something as small as a merit badge.

Perhaps you remember the children's story about the "warm fuzzies" and "cold pricklies?" "Warm fuzzies" made people feel loved and encouraged while "cold pricklies" made them feel unwanted and alienated. Many businesses are filled with people who give each other cold pricklies. Usually this comes from the top down. I once was hired to give seminars on customer service to postal service window clerks. I gave a number of seminars and finally realized that I was not doing much good. One window clerk said it best,

"How can you expect us to give out "warm fuzzies" when all we get from our supervisors is "cold pricklies?""

The problem today with many business owners and managers is they simply do not understand this principle. Their idea of reinforcement is negative criticism.

As indicated earlier, the Drill Sergeant tries to motivate people through put-downs, criticism, and sarcasm. The Buddy-Buddy chooses to say nothing, which is possibly as damaging, if not more s o, than the negative remark.

The Leader, on the other hand, understands the importance of positive recognition of his employees. He also understands that what he recognizes often gets repeated to the point of becoming a regular practice in the business. Consider the message of the following story:

A fisherman was fishing in a boat on a lake. All of a sudden, he heard a knock at the side of his boat. He looked and saw a snake with a frog in its mouth. The fisherman immediately felt sorry for the frog, reached down and pulled it out of the snakes' mouth and threw the frog safely over to another part of the lake. He then felt sorry for the snake because he had robbed it of its lunch. All he had in his boat was a bottle of whiskey. So, he took the whiskey and gave the snake two shots. The snake swam away and the fisherman went back to fishing. A few minutes later, he heard another knock at the side of his boat. When he looked over he saw the same snake. But this time he had two frogs in its mouth!

This story isn't really about frogs and snakes and I'm not comparing our coworkers to snakes. It is about rewards and recognition. As managers of people we get what we reward and recognize. And we need to be careful that we are not rewarding the kinds of behavior we do not want repeated. The Drill Sergeant recognizes poor behavior. What he rewards is compliance and submission. This discourages creativity and initiative because people are afraid of making mistakes. The Buddy-Buddy, because of his leniency, rewards and thereby encourages irresponsibility. The Leader recognizes the importance of reinforcing positive behavior, knowing that what is rewarded will become repeated behavior. Recognition can take the form of verbal praise or something tangible, like a certificate or plaque. A friend of mine who works for a large company told me about a recognition program he implemented. When a coworker went out of his or her way to help someone else with a work-related activity or was especially helpful in dealing with a customer, he gave him or her a certificate worth $5 redeemable at a local video store. He also gave movie tickets and coupons for a free CD. He said, "This cost very little compared to the morale and motivation it produced."

Another company has a weekly drawing with prizes that coworkers can win. Every time a coworker is caught going the extra mile or reaching a goal, a coupon with their name on it is put in the drawing. Prizes range from gift certificates to cash. Workers in this company are very motivated. Some managers provide a periodic lunch for coworkers. Others have an occasional party to recognize team contributions.

Here are three keys to recognizing the contributions of your coworkers.

Key #1 – What is positive reinforcement to one person may not be positive to another.

This places a great responsibility upon managers to get to know their coworkers. While most people respond positively to verbal praise, others want something tangible like a certificate of recognition, a plaque, and not surprisingly, money. Money may be the root of all evil but people love it! And our coworkers need it! Money is a powerful motivator to the coworker of the new millennium and it can take many forms -- a bonus, an increase in pay, a day off with pay, or even a gift certificate.

Money is important to people in another way. For example, it is a symbol of how much a person is worth. How often does one person ask another, "How much do you make?" Consider the psychological impact on an entry-level worker, for example, who makes *more* than minimum wage. It says to her that her employer values her. Many business owners are short sighted in this area. They say, "I'll cut labor costs and save a lot of money." They cut expenses and end up cutting their throat by losing good people. It may be worth the investment of one or two dollars more an hour to communicate to coworkers that they are important and valued. When coworkers feel valued, they usually respond with loyalty and greater productivity.

How do you find out what motivates your coworkers? Ask them! You might say something like this at the time of hiring.

> *"I like to reward my people for going the extra mile. The extra mile could be filling in for a coworker who is sick. Staying late to help customers. Taking the initiative to stay busy and find things to do. Or arriving to work consistently early. These rewards range from a cash bonus, or a day off with pay, to a gift certificate. Which do you prefer?"*

I found that when I did this, the new coworker immediately perked up. Why? Because he knew three things: first, that I expected him to be successful; second, that I was prepared to reward him; and third, that I meant business. Contrast this with telling new coworkers everything that will happen if they mess up. People often will rise or fall to our expectations. A friend of mine, while visiting the East Coast ,found a small child's boat floating on the water. On the side of the boat was written, "Accept your limitations and they are yours."

Key #2 – Recognizing employee contributions requires constant effort.

It is easy in today's business environment to get into a negativity rut. What I mean by this is that all we see is the negative. Have you noticed that negativity generally produces negativity? I have to constantly remind myself to look for the positive things my coworkers do. Sometimes that requires a lot of looking! But positive things can be found. For example, a coworker is habitually late, but provides excellent customer service. If we can focus on the positive and praise the good behavior, we create an atmosphere wherein the coworker is more motivated to change the poor behavior. I'm not suggesting here that we let negative behavior go unnoticed. But often this is all we notice! If we have a rock in our shoe, we might focus on the rock so much that we miss the beauty of the day.

One thing that has helped me to focus on the good things my coworkers do is to post a card that says,

"Recognize Contributions," and make sure I post it where I can see it every day.

Key #3 – Recognizing employee contributions doesn't mean we neglect correcting employees.

While the Drill Sergeant is a master at correcting people, the Buddy-Buddy hates it. I have had many managers tell me this is the most distasteful part of their job and they avoid it at all costs.

The Leader understands that he is in the business of developing people and that the correction of a coworker's behavior is absolutely essential.

What we hesitate to do now, we often pay for later, with interest! This is an "avoidance syndrome", which is the problem of most "Buddy-Buddies." They know what should be done but avoid doing it because it is painful. Consider the example of a mechanic telling a car owner that his car needs a new transmission that will cost $1200. The owner says, "That's a lot of money." The mechanic replies, "You can pay me now or you can pay me later, but it will be twice as much because you will have to add towing and the additional damage that will occur!"

The Leader also understands that the <u>way</u> he corrects behavior is important. Ranting and raving, the style of the Drill Sergeant, is counter-productive. Correction should be done in a civil and reasonable manner, where respect for the coworker is communicated. Remember, you want cooperation as well as compliance. Compliance is sometimes an illusion. The coworker may say, "I will," but really means, "I'll show you, you _____ _____ _____!"

I use a graduated system of correction. Most problems, if they are not corrected through positive reinforcement, receive a verbal reminder. If the behavior is repeated, I sit down with the person and discuss the problem, clearly explaining the consequences. The consequences range from a written report that goes in his or her file, to a reduction in work hours, to termination.

L.L. Steinmetz has suggested "seven deadly sins" a manager needs to avoid when correcting an employee.

1. Failing to obtain all the relevant facts and disciplining based on only hearsay evidence.

2. Disciplining the employee when one is emotionally out of control. This entails losing ones' temper and "flying off the handle."

3. Failing to let the employee know the precise reason he or she is being disciplined.

4. Failing to get the employee's side of the story and not letting him or her talk.

5. Letting the employee talk you out of the punishment that should rightly be invoked.

6. Failing to document what transpires during the disciplinary interview.

7. Holding a grudge against the employee after the disciplinary interview and reminding him or her either verbally or non-verbally about it.

To this list I would add an eighth.

8. Disciplining a coworker in front of customers or other coworkers.

I've known managers who went out of their way to embarrass coworkers in front of other people. What is wrong with this? First, it often embarrasses the customer, too, and creates a bad impression of the business. Second, it humiliates the coworker in front of others. The coworker will then hold a grudge and focus his energy on getting back at his manager.

Remember this: recognizing the contributions of coworkers is a form of compensation. And it's not taxed!

Chapter 7 Summary

- Recognition of coworkers is as important as their paycheck.

- What is recognized usually gets repeated.

- Leaders understand how their coworkers like to be recognized.

- Leaders do not neglect to discipline their coworkers.

Chapter 8

C

A

R

Earn Trust

S

Principle: Trust is not automatic;
it is something that must be earned.

One day a coworker asked to speak with me in private. We went to the office and she said the following, " I really like the new manager. I can always count on what he says!"

There is one quality of a Leader that is perhaps more important than all others, a quality that will gain the respect and trust of coworkers. This quality is credibility. The root word is from the Latin "credo" which refers to a set of beliefs or principles. Leaders are people who live by a set of values and principles, such that people can count on them! Because of their credibility, coworkers trust their manager.

A manager's position gives him authority, but his behavior <u>earns</u> respect and trust. I have found four qualities of a Leader that earn trust.

Honesty and Trustworthiness

One of the most frequent complaints I hear from people about their manager is "He says one thing and does another!" Some managers I have known tell people what they think they want to hear with no intention of following through. I worked as vice president of a company where I spent half of my time flying around the country cleaning up the false promises and expectations the President had communicated.

Edward R. Murrow, journalist and news commentator, put it this way: "To be persuasive we must be believable; to be believable, we must be credible, to be credible, we must be truthful."

Barry Kuzos in his extensive studies on what people look for in leaders wrote: "The most important quality of a leader is honesty across the board."

I have tried in my relationships with coworkers to never make promises I could not keep or to say things I did not mean. Sometimes it is a challenge to be trustworthy and credible, but it is the only way to build respect and to earn trust.

Another element of credibility is to communicate a sense of trust in our coworkers. Research has shown that the leaders with the lowest credibility were the most controlling. People who are controlling communicate a lack of trust in their coworkers. This is the reason Drill Sergeants are not trusted by their coworkers. Drill Sergeants do not trust them!

A Leader understands the importance of proper delegation in communicating trust. I have heard managers say, "If I want something done, I have to do it myself!"

I believe that most coworkers can learn and grow if we know how to properly delegate. This will be discussed in Chapter 9, "Strengthen Coworkers."

Set the example

A Leader is an example of what she asks her coworkers to do. One manager who I consider to be a Leader put it this way: " I try to motivate my coworkers by being an example to them of what I want them to do. I get to work before they do. I stay later than they do. I want them to see that I am willing to do what I ask them to do."

Fairness and Consistency

Do you remember the term "teacher's pet?" This referred to the student other students felt the teacher favored. Managers also have their "pets." This is normal and natural because we all have people whom we like more than others. However, what is destructive is when managers are either unfair or inconsistent in their treatment of their coworkers. Parents understand this principle very well. Children demand fairness! "You treat John better than you do me!" We simply cannot trust someone we believe is unfair.

How do you exhibit fairness and consistency? Establish a set of coworker rules with a discipline policy. Explain this clearly to each coworker and then seek to administer the policy the same way to *all* coworkers. As you strive to do this, coworkers will feel they can count on you!

Experience and Competency

Have you ever had a teacher who was not competent in the subject being taught? How much trust would you have in a surgeon who had just squeaked by in medical school? Would you trust your car to someone who you knew had ruined three other cars?

People just seem to trust people who are competent. Competency refers to our ability to do what we are asking our coworkers to do. If they have a problem, they can count on us to help them.

Sometimes people try to fake it. This works for a while but soon people figure out what is going on. Managers need to be competent in most areas of their business. One area I have found to be the most neglected is that of dealing with people -- coworkers and customers. For some reason we think that being given the title "manager" automatically makes us competent. The number one problem in American business today is troubled relationships between managers and their coworkers.

Most people who are dissatisfied with their job are really dissatisfied with their manager or supervisor. How do I know this? I have talked with hundreds of workers who have told me, "This job would be great if it were not for my boss!"

Drill Sergeants and Buddy-Buddy's need to step up to the plate and make the necessary changes to build credibility and trust with their coworkers. How does one go about making these changes? First, remember that becoming a Leader is a process. You can do it! Second, evaluate your strengths and weaknesses. If you have the courage, you can get feedback from your coworkers. Or, you can use the evaluation at the end of this chapter as a guide. Third, focus on one area of improvement. Attend a seminar on this area. Read a book about it. Talk with someone who has the skill you want. Ask for their help.

And don't be afraid to ask coworkers for their help. Showing that we recognize areas wherein we need help builds trust.

And, finally, make a concerted effort to acquire this new skill or attitude.

Now let's review. Trust is earned when we are credible and is based on:

- Honesty and trustworthiness.
- Being an example.
- Fairness and consistency
- Experience and competency

Remember, credibility is to our coworkers what quality is to our customers.

Chapter 8 Summary

• Leaders earn the respect and trust of their coworkers.

• Leaders do not expect their coworkers to do what they are not willing to do.

• Effective Leaders are honest, fair, and competent.

• Becoming an effective leader is a process: it can be learned.

Coworker Feedback – Tell Us What You Think

Please answer the following questions by circling either "Strongly Agree" (SA), "Agree" (A), "Uncertain" (U), "Disagree" (D), or "Strongly Disagree" (SD).

1. SA A U D SD   My manager cares about me and about my success.

2. SA A U D SD   My manager shares adequate information with me about the business.

3. SA A U D SD   My manager has explained clearly to me the priorities of my job.

4. SA A U D SD   I know who my immediate supervisor is.

5. SA A U D SD   My manager communicates in a positive way with me.

6. SA A U D SD   My manager shows respect and courtesy to me.

7. SA A U D SD   My manager listens to me.

8. SA A U D SD   I feel I have adequate opportunity to communicate my ideas and feelings to my manager.

9. SA A U D SD   I feel that our company provides an important service to people.

10. SA A U D SD   My manager has a goal for our business.

11. SA A U D SD   My manager helps me understand why certain tasks I am asked to do are important.

12. SA A U D SD   We have team goals in our company.
13. SA A U D SD   My manager helps me set personal goals for my job.
14. SA A U D SD   My manager adequately recognizes the contributions I make to the company.
15. SA A U D SD   My manager usually says nothing when I do something good.
16. SA A U D SD   I feel my manager appreciates what I do.
17. SA A U D SD   My manager disciplines coworkers in a proper manner.
18. SA A U D SD   My manager loses his/her temper when upset.
19. SA A U D SD   My manager plays favorites.
20. SA A U D SD   I can count on what my manager says.
21. SA A U D SD   I trust my manager.
22. SA A U D SD   My manager sets a proper example of what he/she expects of us.
23. SA A U D SD   My manager delegates well.
24. SA A U D SD   My manager is knowledgeable and competent in this business.
25. SA A U D SD   I like my manager.
26. SA A U D SD   My manager is always learning and growing.
27. SA A U D SD   My manager encourages me when I make mistakes.
28. SA A U D SD   I have been trained well for my job.
29. SA A U D SD   My manager provides ongoing training to help me with my job.

30. SA A U D SD   My manager shows an interest in my ability to do my job well.
31. SA A U D SD   There is a positive work environment in our company.
32. SA A U D SD   I enjoy working here.
33. SA A U D SD   Some of my coworkers take advantage of our manager.
34. SA A U D SD   Most coworkers waster a lot of time.
35. SA A U D SD   I am motivated to do my best with this job.

If I were the manager I would change . . .

Chapter 9

C

A

R

E

Strengthen Coworkers

Principle: Leaders develop their coworkers.

One of the ways to meet our coworkers' need for self-worth is to assist them with their growth and development. When people accomplish something, they feel better about themselves. Ken Blanchard put an interesting twist on his statement "People who feel good about themselves produce good results." He said, "People who produce good results feel good about themselves." Competent, effective people are the ones who receive praise and are rewarded. The more competent our workers are, the more productive they will be in their jobs. Leaders understand this and realize they are in the business of not just managing things, but developing people.

Here are six suggestions for developing coworkers.

Suggestion #1 – Grow and Develop Yourself

It is difficult to raise another to higher ground if we are not first standing there ourselves. Someone has observed, "What you do speaks so loudly I cannot hear what you say." Leaders are constantly seeking to improve and develop their own skills. They are the example. This is what distinguishes a leader from a follower. When a Leader is growing and improving, he is then able to ask and help his coworkers do the same. There is possibly nothing more pathetic than a person who has stopped growing. This is a grand key to helping ourselves and our coworkers avoid burnout. We need to constantly provide them with opportunities for growth and development. And we will not do this unless we are doing it ourselves! So, how do we become the model? Here are some ideas:

1. Learn a new skill.

2. Attend workshops and seminars.

3. Read books that address critical areas of leadership.

4. Take a course on leadership at a local college or even on-line.

5. Get feedback from your coworkers.

6. Spend more time reflecting and evaluating your leadership performance.

7. Develop a new hobby – anything that makes life more interesting.

8. Write a book or an article on what you have learned in being a business owner or manager.

To grow we must constantly be involved in something that is growing us.

Suggestion #2 – Encourage Your Coworkers

Like us, our coworkers have many challenges and problems in their lives. These are a result of the four needs discussed in Chapter 3. They may have trouble meeting their physical needs. Relationships may turn sour. They sometimes feel that fun and variety is missing in their lives. They bring these problems to work and we see the results in their lack of motivation and unsatisfactory performance.

The Drill Sergeant adds to their problems by deflating self-worth through put downs and insensitivity. His idea of encouragement is to increase the pressure. The Buddy-Buddy attempts to relieve pressure by offering sympathy but usually gives no real help. The Leader supports coworkers by knowing how and when to give needed encouragement.

John Maxwell reported an experiment that was conducted to measure people's capacity to endure pain. "Psychologists measured how long a barefooted person could stand in a bucket of ice water. They found that one factor made it possible for some people to stand in the ice water twice as long as others. Can you guess what that factor was? It was encouragement. The sufferers were able to endure pain much longer than their unencouraged counterparts."

This is probably why the Lamaze childbirth program is so successful. It makes childbirth a team effort, with one giving the other needed encouragement and support.

How do Leaders encourage their coworkers? They use positive rather than negative words.

People have what might be called an emotional bank account. Every time we say something negative we make a withdrawal. Every time we encourage and compliment them we make a deposit. You might check sometime to see whether the emotional bank accounts of your coworkers are overdrawn.

Leaders, as pointed out in Chapter 5, are sensitive to their choice of words.

They show confidence in their coworkers.

One way to do this is to give coworkers tasks and responsibilities. Leaders are constantly searching for ways to grow their coworkers.

They are generous in their praise.

For example, words like "okay," and "not bad" may not communicate to a coworker that you are pleased with them.

A compliment paid six months ago may have little value to a coworker in need of appreciation today. Some people are generous with praise; others are stingy. Those who are stingy rarely realize they are. What does it cost to praise coworkers? The story is told of a woman who said to her husband, "You haven't told me recently that you loved me!" He replied, "I told you fifteen years ago I loved you. If that changes I'll let you know!" Be generous in your praise! I witnessed firsthand this kind of leader. I was in his hotel at 8 in the morning just as his new housekeeping team arrived for their shift. He gave each a "high five", greeting them by name and encouraging each one. This leader was a cheerleader of his team!

Suggestion #3 – Give Them the Tools to do Their Job Effectively

One of the most common complaints of managers is "My employees don't do their job correctly!" Often the problem is not as much with the coworker as it is with the manager or supervisor who has not trained them properly. If coworkers have been trained properly, the manager or supervisor needs to make it clear the coworker can come to them with any questions.

Proper, effective training is one of the most essential elements of motivation. People need to know how to do their job. Knowing how to do their job is essential to strengthening self-worth.

Because people have different backgrounds and work experience, the Leader assesses coworkers' training needs. How is this done? First, treat each coworker as an individual. Be careful of assumptions and stereotypes. Just because someone has a college degree doesn't mean she will be successful at a job. Likewise, because a person has little formal education does not mean he cannot be excellent at certain jobs.

Second, know the specific skills coworkers will need to accomplish their job. For example, a coworker who is hired as a grocery clerk might need to be able to do the following:

- Deal with customers in a professional way.
- Know the layout of the store.
- Understand and be able to use the register.
- Know how to count money.

Third, assume they have <u>never</u> been trained in the skills they need to be successful at their job. Why? Because even if they have been trained, they may have been trained improperly. I interviewed a young man for a position in one of our restaurants and he said, "You're going to love me!" I asked "why?" He responded, "Because I've worked in a business just like yours!" I knew immediately this was a potential red flag. And I was right! Don't depend on someone else's training. A story is told of Vince Lombardi, the famous coach of the Green Bay Packers. He began every summer training session by holding up a football (remember, how many of his players wore super bowl rings) and saying, "Gentlemen, this is a football! I am going to assume you know nothing about football." He would then retrain all of his players on the fundamentals of the game. During half time of a game where they were behind by two touchdowns, he was shown how difficult it is to train people. He held up a football and said, "Gentlemen, this is a football!" One of his linemen said, "Not so fast coach!"

You probably shouldn't complain about high turnover if you have paid only lip service to training!

Fourth, train your coworkers the way you want them trained. Proper training has a huge impact on reducing turnover, especially in the first few weeks of employment. Most people, left to themselves without proper training and supervision, will choose to do a job quickly rather than well. The following four steps, when applied consistently, will not only save you time later on, but will ensure that coworkers do things the way you want them done.

The steps are:

- Give trainees a written checklist for important tasks.
- Assign someone to walk them through the checklist.
- Give immediate feedback.
- Continue on-going praise, encouragement, and retraining.

Each of these steps is necessary to have an adequately trained coworker. Because of time, you will be tempted to take shortcuts. Simply showing or telling coworkers how to do something and then leaving them on their own to accomplish it is not enough. Skipping steps may save time initially; but, in the long run, it might cost you more to correct mistakes and retrain a coworker.

Step 1 – Give the trainee a written checklist for important tasks.

People learn differently. Some learn best by hearing, others by seeing. A written checklist shows the trainee a step-by-step procedure for important tasks. I have had more success with checklists than I have had with any other training method. A checklist shows the trainee exactly how you want something done. I have checklists for answering the business telephone, for greeting customers, for handling complaints, and for taking or refunding a customer's money. To accomplish this, you need to know what specific skills your coworkers need to be successful at their job. Here is an example of a checklist for greeting customers developed by a major California supermarket:

- Say "Welcome to _____. How is your day going?"
- Ask them if they found everything they needed.
- Ask them if they have our grocery card. If they do not, explain that it will save them money.
- Ring their order up and show the customer on the receipt how much money they saved shopping with us.

Step 2 – Assign someone to walk them through the checklist.

Because training is so important, I either do much of it myself or have one of our best coworkers assigned as our trainer. The trainer can model how to do a specific task and then have the trainee do it under supervision. The only way you can tell if a coworker understands how to do a job is by having someone watch him or her do it. This also gives the trainee a chance to ask questions.

Step 3 – Give immediate feedback.

Most trainees want to know what they are doing right and what they are doing wrong. This step in the training process is very important because feedback will help them start off right. Bad habits learned up-front are much harder to change later on. But take note. It is not enough to give new team members their initial training with lots of feedback, and then let them go on their own. Studies show that people forget much of what they hear the first time through. One owner exclaimed to another more experienced owner, "How many times do I need to tell my coworkers something?" The owner responded, "I guess as many times as it takes for them to learn it!" Immediate feedback is important while the actions of the coworker are fresh in their mind.

One caution; be careful not to be too harsh or critical. People are usually very sensitive to criticism, especially when learning something new. Here are key points to remember when giving feedback:

Tell the trainee early in the process that you understand that we all make mistakes and that mistakes are valuable learning lessons. You may want to share some personal experiences.

When the trainee does something correctly, give immediate positive reinforcement. "You did a great job on that."

Here's a statement that reinforces correct behavior and adds a follow up component. "You did it exactly right that time. Keep up the good work."

When trainees do something incorrectly, give specific suggestions as to how they should do the job. Notice the difference in the following two corrections:

"You missed this."

"One of the easiest things to miss is... Let me show you how to correct that."

Should a trainee become defensive by making excuses simply say, "Let's not worry about what happened. Show me how you did it." Then say, "OK, now I see. Here's how I want it done." Avoid getting in a debate, which only wastes time and may encourage defensiveness. Remember, the goal is not to win an argument, but to improve performance.

Step 4 – Provide on-going praise, encouragement, and retraining.

Why is this important? Because much of the learning and growth coworkers will experience is while they are doing the job. Somebody needs to be there following up. Coworkers must be looked at as being apprentices. We cannot assume that initial instructions are enough. What success will a gardener have who plants seeds and then fails to water and weed later on?

Much of the success you have in training your team members is dependent on your positive approach to feedback. Taking a positive approach with team members is an on-going, every hour, every day commitment. Coworkers will have greater success developing their job skills when their training is enhanced with on-going praise, encouragement, and retraining.

Perceive yourself as a constant trainer, one who is always looking for opportunities to help your coworkers grow and develop.

Suggestion #4 – Be accessible to your coworkers

Leaders are out among their coworkers making themselves accessible for questions. They are also out among their coworkers to assess needs and challenges. Leadership is not only about sitting in the office; it's about working with and developing people.

Suggestion #5 – Delegate what you can to coworkers

In Chapter 8, I indicated that when we delegate to coworkers we show trust and confidence in them. The delegation of tasks has at least three purposes:

- To encourage their growth and development.
- To engender trust within coworkers. When we trust them, they usually, in turn, trust us.
- To free-up time for the manager.

To accomplish the first purpose, we need to be effective at delegating. Note that I have placed the manager's convenience last for a purpose. Delegation should not be thought of primarily as a way to relieve the manager's workload. It is to develop coworkers.

Effective delegation is not simply giving a coworker an assignment and leaving them to do it. The following keys are absolutely necessary to help them in their growth.

- Pick the right coworker for the right task. People are usually better at some things than they are others.
- Clearly explain what you want done and what the desired outcome is.
- Note the difference in the following:

"I want you to clean the floor."

"I would like you to clean the floor so that our customers can see their reflection in it."

- Give the coworker the proper tools to accomplish the task.

- Set up a specific time to evaluate how they are doing.

The evaluation can be as important as any of the four steps. Here is where you have an opportunity to really train the coworker. This is particularly true if the task is to be repeated.

If a coworker experiences problems, help the coworker find a solution. Often, managers step in and solve the problems their coworkers have. Help them become self-reliant and empowered by asking them: "What do you think should be done?" "Here are some alternatives. Which do you think is the best?"

By proper delegation, we assist our coworkers in growing and developing. This, in turn, increases their self worth and helps them feel a part of the team.

Suggestion #6 – Conduct regular performance reviews of coworkers

Tom Peters says, "The number one leadership skill is the ability to develop others. That's not a new idea. But boss, check your calendar: How much time are you devoting <u>directly</u> to people-development? One colleague at Apple computer formally dedicated 100 days a year to what, with a smile, he calls 'performance reviews.'"

A performance review offers a manager a number of opportunities:

- An opportunity to receive information on how the coworker is feeling about his or her job.
- An opportunity to share information, to encourage, praise, and give direction.
- An opportunity to set goals.

Two questions are very effective when conducting performance reviews"

    1. "How are you feeling about your job?"

    2. "What can I do to help?"

These two questions usually open the door to a very meaningful discussion. What does a performance review do for coworkers?

- It says that the manager cares.
- It gives coworkers a chance to express feelings, thus increasing self-worth.
- It gives coworkers encouragement to continue to do their best.

Chapter 9 Summary

- Leaders develop people, not just manage programs.

- Encourage your coworkers – be their greatest cheerleader!

- The Leader's responsibility to train begins at the time of hiring and continues throughout the coworker's employment.

- Leaders delegate, not just for his or her own convenience, but also for the growth of their coworkers.

- Leaders constantly monitor the growth of their coworkers through interviews and performance reviews.

Chapter 10

Putting CARES to Work

to Motivate and Retain Coworkers

Principle: Leaders make it happen!

I visit regularly with managers from every type of business. They all have the same two major problems: 1) motivating their coworkers to do what they have been trained to do, and, 2) retaining good people.

Let's look at how applying the CARES principles discussed in the preceding chapters can assist with both of these challenges.

Motivating Coworkers

Here is an example from a manager of a fast food restaurant, "How do I get my employees to treat my customers right?"

Communicate Effectively

- Make sure the person you have hired is a "fit " for customer service.
- Explain at the time of hiring how you want your customers treated. Make sure the new coworkers clearly understands your expectations.

Acts with Purpose

- Attach a customer service result to every task you want the coworker to do.
- Set a goal with the coworker relative to customer service. For example, learn the product line within the first week so as to be able to assist customers.

Recognizes Contributions

- Try and catch the coworker doing things right. Give verbal praise and encouragement

Earns Trust

- Be an example to coworkers of excellent customer service.

Strengthens Coworkers

- Assign an experienced coworker to the trainee.
- Give the trainee a customer service checklist.
- Give ongoing coaching to the trainee.
- Review the coworker's performance within three to four weeks.

Retaining Good People

Most business owners and managers are concerned with turnover. Let's apply CARES to this challenge. Remember, when coworkers like their job, they are more likely to stay with it.

Communicates Effectively

- Build a positive work environment by showing respect and concern for coworkers.
- Keep coworkers informed on business and industry updates.
- Make time to listen to the concerns and feelings of coworkers.

Acts with Vision and Purpose

- Creates a team feeling having coworkers give input into team goals.

Recognizes Contribution

- Learn what motivates each of your coworkers.
- Make sure coworkers receive timely raises and bonuses.
- Try and catch your coworkers doing things right.
- Create a fun atmosphere by providing a lunch or a party from time to time.
- Avoid disciplining coworkers improperly.

Earns Trust

- Follow through with what you say you will do.
- Be fair and consistent with coworkers.

Strengthen Coworkers

- Make sure coworkers have the tools to do the job.
- Develop an effective training program.
- Be accessible to your coworkers.
- Delegate tasks to strengthen coworkers.

Nearly every problem you face with your coworkers can be addressed by using the CARES principle. But, how do you know how successful you have been? I have a friend who says "Measure it, or forget it". There are four measurements you can use.

1. Turnover. Because of your efforts has turnover been reduced?
2. Customer complaints. Have customer complaints gone down?

3. Sales increase. Because of your leadership have sales gone up?

4. Coworker feedback. Do coworkers rate you as an effective manager?

Chapter 10 Summary

- Leaders apply the correct principles to affect coworker behavior.

- The two major challenges managers face is coworker motivation and retention of good people.

- CARES can assist with each of these challenges.

Chapter 11

Building a Positive Work Environment

Principle: A positive workplace
creates happy coworkers.

One of the most essential ingredients to the retention of coworkers is a positive work environment. Next to money, the workplace is probably the most important aspect of the job. This also helps prevent burnout. We have already discussed how the attitude and style of the manager affects the work environment. Let's look at two other factors that help create a positive workplace.

Create Variety and Fun

Anything you can do to give coworkers a variety of experiences will increase job satisfaction. We can't assume that money is the sole criteria that determines whether a person likes a job. There are some people who work for less than what they could earn elsewhere because of the way they are treated and how much they enjoy their job. Some jobs lend themselves to variety much better than do others. Also, some people become bored more quickly than do others. How do we deal with this?

Help coworkers see how the job will benefit them in the future. You must know your people to do this. Help them see their job in terms of not only immediate, but long term benefits.

Many jobs are routine and even mind-numbing. This may not be helped but we can still look for opportunities to give coworkers a change in what they are doing. The change may be for a day or even an hour in running an errand. Sometimes a short change in routine can make a difference. It can also help them learn a new skill. Remember, you're working with people, not machines!

Do things periodically that are different from the normal work experience. For example, establish a Friday casual day where coworkers do not have to dress as they normally do; or, a weekly lunch where coworkers eat together. A party one evening every two or three months to relax and have fun. Dress up for holidays such as Halloween. Decorate the office or store on special holidays.

Staff competition can be a way of having fun while increasing productivity:

- Hold a Saturday softball game or barbecue.
- One department or group of coworkers could challenge another group to a contest.

Prevent and Resolve Coworker Conflicts

Often, the number one reason for a negative work environment is conflicts between coworkers. Conflicts are normal and natural in life and in the workplace. They can actually be beneficial if they lead to improvements. However, when conflict affects team morale and productivity, leaders need to step in and help solve the problem. Unresolved conflicts almost inevitably lead to an unhappy staff.

As owners and managers we can't become so caught up in the mechanics of our business that we overlook the very people who make it work. If a business fails, it is often because of people problems, not because of system failures.

Unfortunately, some managers approach team conflicts in one of two ways. To avoid hurting feelings or elevating the level of the conflict, the Buddy-Buddy avoids intervening. Typically, we'll hear the Buddy-Buddy say something like, "Let's all try and get along." In contrast, the Drill Sergeant uses warnings and threats and says things like, "Either you two get along or you're out of here!" Usually, neither of these approaches will usually solve the problem and may actually make the conflict worse.

Why do Conflicts Occur?

As a leader-manager, understanding why conflicts occur and knowing their cause can assist you in preventing conflict before it happens and in dealing with it when it does. Team conflict is a complex issue and there are many reasons for it. The most common reasons for conflict are:

Behavioral traits. Habits and attitudes have a profound impact on how people function at a job and how they relate with other people. For example, a coworker with a happy-go-lucky attitude might have some conflict with a serious, get-down-to-business person. Some one who enjoys the out-of-doors might have a conflict with someone who enjoys staying at home watching television. Common attitudes and habits that create conflict are negativity, moodiness, a short temper, impatience, not being punctual, an abrasive personality, and disrespect for authority.

Professional Jealousy. We live in a very competitive world. Some coworkers may think they should be a manager or supervisor because they can do the job better, thus creating conflict. A successful worker, however, has learned to accept direction and respects those who exercise leadership.

Differing Work Habits.   People work at different speeds and often have different ideas as to how a job should be done. For example, it is extremely frustrating for a coworker who is fast and efficient to work with one who is slow and methodical. Cultural differences may also produce different approaches and perceptions of job tasks.

Family Stress. Because people ultimately bring to their job the problems and stresses they have in their homes, they may be more irritable and difficult to work with.

Conflicting Viewpoints. Conflict results from differences in opinion, perspective, personality, values, etc. For example, a coworker who follows policy to the letter might come in conflict with one who likes to bend the rule.

"Better Than Thou" Attitude.   Most coworkers find it difficult to work with someone who conveys the impression of being better than they are or of being always right. They may exhibit harsh, dictatorial, or prejudiced behaviors that are demeaning and insensitive.

What Are Some Warning Signs of Conflict?

As an owner or manager charged with the responsibility of helping coworkers resolve conflicts, you need to be sensitive to warning signs that conflict may be occurring. Sometimes coworkers are reluctant to say anything about a problem. Here are some common warning signs.

The coworker is sullen, withdrawn, or not as friendly or happy as usual, or becomes more vocal, abusive, and short tempered.

A coworker starts missing work and/or is habitually late.

Work that is usually done well is not done correctly or is done in a sloppy manner.

A coworker alerts you to a problem.

What Are the Consequences of Conflict to Your Business?

Some owners/managers choose to do little when it comes to resolving conflicts between coworkers. Their attitude is "With time it will all work out." The problem with this attitude is simple: what happens between the time the conflict occurs and its resolution? Should conflicts be allowed to continue, you may experience one or more of the following negative results:

Conflict is contagious. When people are upset, they usually seek out others to support them. This results in other coworkers taking sides, which expands the conflict beyond the few involved.

Coworker morale is affected negatively. One of the most important ingredients of job enjoyment is how coworkers interact with each other. Job conflict leads to unhappy employees, which affects coworker morale, and may result in loss of good people. This ultimately affects your customers and your ability to meet their needs.

Productivity is reduced. Conflict diverts attention from the job that needs to be done and reduces the quality of work.

Communication between coworkers is weakened. Conflict and anger often produce silence and irrational or volatile behaviors, at the very time when communication is most needed. When communication ceases, coworkers stop working effectively together.

What Can You Do to Prevent Conflicts Before They Occur?

It has been said, "An ounce of prevention is worth a pound of cure." So it is with coworker conflict. If you can prevent conflict from occurring, you will save time, energy, and hurt feelings between coworkers.

To prevent coworker conflict you must take action *before* the conflict occurs.

Here are some suggestions. At the time of hiring or orientation, or in a staff meeting:

- Explain to your coworkers that whining, backbiting, and gossiping are unacceptable behavior.

- Explain that should they have a problem with a coworker, they should first go to that person to try and work it out.

- Explain who they should go to if that doesn't work.

- Explain that if they come to you for help they should come with a solution.

- Explain to new coworkers how you expect them to manage family illness, emergencies, and personal appointments. Be sensitive to individual coworker issues and consistently reinforce and enforce your expectations.

Some other suggestions are:

- Train coworkers in how to resolve differences using the guidelines outlined in this chapter.
- Model and foster an environment where all members feel they can contribute and are valued for what they offer the organization. Recognize everyone's contribution, both individually and as a group. Do not tolerate behaviors, even from high performers, that belittle others, or are harsh, dictatorial, or prejudiced. Be fair in your administration of discipline.

What Are Some Roadblocks to Resolving Conflicts?

Even though you do everything you can to prevent conflict from happening, it will happen. The hiring interview does not always reveal future personality problems or conflicts. When conflict occurs, you must step in and help mediate a resolution. Before conflicts can be resolved, you need to be aware of the roadblocks that affect a positive resolution.

Roadblocks Caused By Coworkers in Conflict:

1. Inability to focus on a solution. Often, people become very emotionally involved in the issue that is creating the conflict. Because emotional behavior is seldom rational, whether positive or negative, there is little if any focus on a solution.

2. Unwillingness to try. The indispensable element in conflict resolution is a willingness and a commitment on the part of both parties to resolve it. You must get commitment up-front from each party that they will try and resolve the issue.

3. Insistence on being right. No one is right all of the time and conflict is seldom one-sided. A person who insists on being right is unable to learn, grow, and resolve problems. Such people will surely have trouble working with others.

4. Lack of information. Most often people in a conflict do not see the full picture. There are two sides to every

issue, sometimes even more, and usually the parties involved do not understand one of these sides.

5. Refusal to forgive and forget. Some people hold grudges. Grudges should have no place at work. They harm both the person to whom they are directed and the person who holds them.

6. Prejudice. Race, age, social background, and religion are common areas that produce prejudice. Although we see ourselves as a country where prejudice is discouraged, it still may produce conflicts.

Roadblocks Caused by the One Mediating the Conflict

The word "mediator" refers to an individual who stands between two people and assists them in coming closer together. You also should be aware of the problems you might create as a mediator.

- Wrong place and wrong time. Timing is very important when resolving conflicts. When team members are tired or emotionally upset, you should probably pick a better time to get them together.

- Pre-judging. Not having all the information can prevent you from making a good decision. Avoid jumping to conclusions before you've heard all the facts or imposing a pet theory on a situation it doesn't fit.

- Showing favoritism. A mediator isn't an advocate for either party in a conflict. Even the appearance of favoritism can block the resolution of a conflict.

- Giving a simplistic solution. Saying to team members, "Shake hands, just forget it" will not usually solve a serious conflict, nor will it satisfy the upset coworkers who expect you to take their problem seriously, not brush it off.

- Doing all the talking. The key role of a mediator is to ask questions and to listen. The purpose of questions is to lead those involved in the conflict to discover how they caused or helped perpetuate the conflict, and how they can be instrumental in resolving it. When the mediator does all of the talking, the participants have no investment in a resolution.

Resolving Conflicts After They Occur

Remember, people in conflict will concentrate on justifying their actions and on giving reasons as to why they are right; not on solving the problem.

Helping team members resolve conflicts is a skill that takes practice and experience to acquire. Anyone who works with people will be involved as a mediator at some time or another. Remember; resolve conflicts as soon as possible. Waiting to resolve conflicts can cause team efforts to break down and even become counter-productive. The key to conflict resolution is to "nip it in the bud" before it has time to become any more serious.

The best approach is to get the two coworkers together. Indicate to them that their behavior is affecting the entire team. Ask for their input. "What do you think the problem is?" Ask each for a solution. If no solution is forthcoming, you might need to offer one. Share the consequences of a positive resolution and the consequences of failure to resolve the issue. This might include a reduction in hours or even termination. Ask each person for a commitment to resolve the issue. Follow-up later to insure they follow through.

Leaders seek to establish a positive work environment by trying to give coworkers variety in their jobs, creating a fun workplace, and by assisting team members to work harmoniously together.

Chapter 11 Summary

• Effective Leaders create a positive work environment.

• Variety and fun help create a positive workplace.

• Leaders work to reduce conflict between coworkers through both prevention and effective mediation.

Chapter 12

Managing People of
Diverse Cultural Backgrounds

Principle: A Leader is sensitive to cultural diversity and sees it
as an opportunity, not as a disadvantage.

In the new millennium, there will be a continuation of
what has happened in the United States since the mid-
twentieth century, that is, the growth of a multi-cultural
workforce. Not only are businesses affected by cultural
diversity among their coworkers, but among their customers,
as well. Businesses will continue to be made up of people
from various national, ethnic, racial and religious
backgrounds. These differences can affect teamwork, job
satisfaction, customer service, and productivity; but the

influence does not need to be negative. This diversity can enrich and enhance the workplace. Can managers treat all of their coworkers the same? Can they recognize the differences and make an effort to understand their coworkers? Can they understand and treat their customers in a positive manner? In this new millennium, capitalizing on diversity will be absolutely essential! The Bureau of Labor Statistics reports that from 1997 to the year 2000 immigrant workers in the U.S. jumped 17 percent. It is estimated that by the year 2020 immigrant workers will make up 20 percent of the workforce!

I have had the opportunity of living outside of the United States for over twelve years. I have also traveled to the Mid-East, Japan, Europe, and Australia. In my businesses, we have employed people from many different cultural backgrounds. Many managers see this as a disadvantage. But it doesn't have to be that way. We need to accept that cultural diversity is a fact in modern society and modern business life. Recognizing this fact, we can look for ways to capitalize on it, rather than complain about it. Here are some key areas that Leaders will want to be aware of, so that they might be prepared to develop coworkers who come from diverse cultures.

Social Values

Various cultures look at such things as work ethic and goals in differing ways. For example, some cultures, like the U.S., are very focused on efficiency and time management. Other cultures may not be as worried about efficiency as they are about relationships with coworkers and customers. Therefore, they are not the ones that will be motivated as much by goals and rewards. The Leader, therefore, finds out where her workers are coming from, i.e., not only their names but also their cultural backgrounds.

Social Behavior

What is polite in one culture could be rude in another. What is considered customer service to one culture may not be the same to another. For example, Americans have a fairly high standard of customer service. We usually expect—even demand—politeness and helpfulness. I believe it was an American who invented the phrase, "The customer is always right." This idea is not a universal standard. In some cultures, business owners have an adversarial relationship with customers.

You need also to be aware of the social backgrounds of the people you hire. In some cultures men look down on women and treat them differently than they do men. Some ethnic groups have ancient grievances or hatreds they may bring into the workplace. While some cultural differences are acceptable, others -- that hurt feelings and turn customers away -- cannot be tolerated. In some cases, special training of coworkers may be required in the form of workshops or individual counseling.

Body Language

One of the greatest lessons I learned living outside of the United States was that body language in one culture may not convey the same meaning as in another. This can be a source of major miscommunication. For example, I found when I was in Japan that a short bow was a sign of respect. Eye contact says to customers in the U.S. that we are interested in them. In some cultures it is a sign of respect

_____

<u>not</u> to look in a person's eyes. Before jumping to conclusions about what the body language of a coworker might mean, make sure you understand his or her cultural background.

Concepts of Time

Some cultures, like that of the U.S., pride themselves on being on time to appointments. In other cultures, time is a relative thing; representatives of such cultures are not as concerned with meeting strict schedules. I have wondered, for example, on trips to the Middle East, why some airline personnel do not get concerned when a flight is late. Here I am jumping up and down because the airplane is not on time and the ticketing agent looks at me as if to say, "What are you upset about? Late is normal."

Unfortunately, in this country, time is of the essence. We are always in a rush, watching the clock, and making sure our palm pilots are in our pocket. The Leader will train his coworkers, no matter what their cultural background, to meet the needs of the customers.

Religious Values

Religion plays a very important role in the lives of many people and customs vary greatly from one religion to another. Leaders seek to understand and respect religious differences. For example, certain religions celebrate specific holidays. Others have prohibitions against certain foods and drinks.

Language Barriers

Even within cultures that speak the same language, there may be differences. My family and I lived in Canada for nine years. On one occasion, while at a friend's for dinner, I asked, "Could I put the napkins on the table? Our host replied, "I believe you mean serviette, napkins are diapers."

Another language barrier exists when we hire coworkers who do not speak good English and we do not speak their language. A mother mouse was trying to teach her offspring the ways of the world when she found herself and family face to face with a great big cat. Her children were terrified. But the mother remained calm and started barking like a dog. The cat heard the barking, turned around, and took off. The mother mouse turned to her little ones and said, "Now you see the importance of a second language!"

Most of us do not have the luxury of a second language. And when we ask coworkers if they understand and speak English, to avoid embarrassment and being fired, they might reply "yes." But in reality they might not understand English that well. We have a lot of slang and idioms they may not understand. Consider what the following might mean to someone who does not completely understand English.

"I want that done ASAP!"

"Make it snappy!"

"That just doesn't cut the mustard."

"Just cool it!"

Leaders are sensitive to language barriers. One company I know, that hires quite a few Hispanic coworkers, offers classes in English for them. That's leadership!

Written Language Barriers

Often business owners and managers communicate with coworkers through newsletters, memos, or letters. If these are not written in a way non-English-speaking coworkers understand, it will have the affect of demoralizing them.

The solution is to have a bilingual coworker write or at least review the memo. Written messages should be short, with simple and clear wording. Slang should be avoided.

Leaders make an effort to learn about their coworkers. They know that when they stereotype people they then do not treat them as individuals. Here are some suggestions for developing intercultural skills.

- Understand clearly what it is you want to communicate.
- Send clear messages that can be easily understood.
- Communicate respect as well as information to your coworkers.
- Check for understanding to ensure that what was communicated was received.
- Be patient and persistent, don't give up.
- Deal with coworkers on an individual basis.

- Try to put yourself in your coworkers' shoes.

Chapter 12 Summary

- Cultural diversity is a fact in the workplace and Leaders regard it as an opportunity rather than a problem.

- Leaders seek to understand the cultural backgrounds of their coworkers.

- Leaders develop inter-cultural skills to capitalize on the strengths of their coworkers.

Chapter 13

Managing Multiple Priorities

Principle: Time spent in planning may save
hours later on.

Most business owners and managers are responsible for multiple priorities. Marketing, customer service, hiring, and finances -- it seems the list is endless. One business owner stood before a judge trying to explain why his business had gone bankrupt. He said, "Your honor, in my company we had a three word philosophy, 'ready, fire, aim.'"

There is nothing so aggravating as to work for a manager or supervisor who is unorganized, who neglects important priorities for less important ones. How many times have you heard someone say the following about such a person: "He flies by the seat of his pants." It is very difficult to work with such people!

Leaders have learned to use their time wisely and to focus on major priorities. And the key is they plan ahead. Peter Drucker has written, "For every minute I spend in planning I save three in execution." Think about that for a minute. If you spend 10 minutes each day planning, it will save you 30 minutes later on.

I have had the opportunity of teaching time management principles all over the world. I have personally seen the change these principles can make in people's lives. Here are seven principles to effectively manage multiple priorities.

Develop a long-range plan for your business.

Where do you want your business to be two years from now? One year? This could be written down in terms of gross sales, profits, or customer base. Leaders have the big picture of their business and its potential.

Break down the long-range plan into a short-term plan.

To reach a long-range objective, we must see the short-term benchmarks. To reach the long-range objectives, where must you be at the end of the first quarter of the first year? The second quarter, and so on?

Determine the most important priorities you should focus on.

The challenge most business owners and managers face is getting caught up in what I call "the thick of thin things." The most important activities we should focus on suffer at the expense of the not so important. For example, critical activities like planning, training, and personal growth get set aside for more urgent things, such as balancing the books.

Alec MacKenzie has written: "Urgency engulfs the manager, yet the most urgent task is not always the most important. The tyranny of the urgent lies in its distortion of priorities. One of the measures of a manager is the ability to distinguish the important from the urgent, to refuse to be tyrannized by the urgent, to refuse to manage by crisis." How do you focus on your most important priorities? Make a list of the most important activities you should focus on as an owner or manager. Then, prioritize these activities. Which ones are critical for you to accomplish?

Delegate

Ask yourself which priorities you could delegate to a coworker. You can't do everything! If you fail to delegate the most important priorities will be neglected.

Plan Weekly

Have you ever come to the end of the day and said to yourself, "I was busy today but what did I accomplish?" Weekly and daily planning is one of the most important habits of organized people. There are three steps to weekly planning.

Step 1- Set aside a 20-30 minute block of time to focus on the coming week. This might be done on Saturday or Sunday.

Step 2- Review all appointments for the coming week making sure the exact time and place are recorded in your planner.

Step 3- Review your list of most important priorities and schedule a time to focus on one or two of them during the week.

Step 4- Record other items on the day of the week you want to accomplish them. This may include telephone calls you want to make, coworkers you want to meet with, and other business, personal, or family items. You now have a skeletal plan for the coming week.

Plan Daily

There are three steps to daily planning

Step 1. Set aside ten to fifteen minutes to plan your day. A good time to do this is early in the morning or the night before.

Step 2. Ask yourself, "What are the most important items I need to focus on today?"

Add these to the other items noted during your weekly planning session.

Step 3. Prioritize each item on your "to do" list. This is a critical step, because it is human nature to focus on the easy or urgent tasks. These may not be the most important priorities.

Important actions such as performance reviews, staff planning, and time for reflection, often get set aside for other urgent things like the telephone and staff interruptions!

One of the ways to prioritize is to quickly weigh each item in the To Do List with an:

A – Must be done

B – Can be done if time

C – can wait

Simply ask this question, "If I don't accomplish anything else today, what must I do?"

Control Interruptions

One of the most persistent problems for managers is constant interruptions. Here are some ideas:

Give coworkers the power to make certain decisions on their own. You must, however, determine when things are to be cleared with you.

Train coworkers that when your door is closed you should only be interrupted for urgent, critical matters.

Put a sign on your door that says, "Only Interrupt with Urgent Items."

Leave the office or business for an hour to concentrate on important items.

Delegate items on your To Do List to your coworkers.

Leaders who fail to plan, plan to fail. It is as simple as that! Poor planning has been the cause of the untimely death of many businesses. Except in rare cases, success isn't an accident, it is the result of effective planning.

Chapter 13 Summary

- Leaders plan long-term as well as short-term.

- Effective planning requires prioritizing tasks and responsibilities.

- Delegate what you can.

- Planning reduces crisis management and wasted time.

SECTION 3

AVOIDING
COSTLY LITIGATION

Chapter 14

Safety and Security Issues

*Principle: A Leader's major concern is a
safe and secure workplace.*

One of the greatest challenges we face as business
owners and managers is the safety of our coworkers and
customers and the security of our businesses. Billions of
dollars are lost each year because of a lack of attention to
these vital areas.

First, let's look at customer and coworker safety. Two
stories will illustrate the importance of a manager's concern
for this area. In one of our stores, we had an outside eating
area. We placed umbrellas in the tables to protect

customers from the sun. The umbrellas were brought into the store at night to avoid theft. In the morning, our opening person was to put the umbrellas out in the tables. One morning the coworker neglected to do so and a customer came into the store to order a sandwich. The umbrellas were still up against the side of the counter. You guessed it! One of the umbrellas fell, striking the customer on the side of the head. After months of doctor and hospital visits, you can imagine the cost of that mistake! Fortunately, I had liability insurance!

A second story happened to a business associate of mine. He had scheduled a young woman to close the store. At eleven at night, a man came into the store, grabbed the young woman, and took her to the back of the store. He raped her and stole what money he could get. The employee sued not only the owner of the store but also the owner of the franchise for neglect in the area of employee safety. Her award was one of the largest ever in that state.

The point of these two stories is evident. As business owners and managers we must be committed to safety. Here are some suggestions:

Customer Safety

The first suggestion is to make sure you have adequate liability insurance. Without this, I would never open my doors for business!

Next, look for places or areas in your business where potential problems are just waiting to happen. It may be slippery floors, poor lighting, objects such as plants that are hanging from the ceiling, or places in the parking lot where customers may trip or fall.

Develop a checklist for employees as to what they should do if a customer has a problem. The key question to ask is, "What could possibly happen to my customers?" Then, make the necessary corrections to see that those things do not happen.

Some businesses even videotape the customer and the injury site. This can be used as evidence, should there be a lawsuit.

Employee Safety

Every industry has common employee safety problems. A safety problem is anything that affects the personal well being of our employees. For example, in the fast food industry the following are common: Skin cuts from knives, meat and vegetable slicers; burns from grills and deep-fat fryers; back problems from lifting inventory; and leg problems from long hours of standing.

Another safety problem that seems to be on the increase is criminal acts. Robbery is one of the most common safety issues in large cities and suburbs. Another area is that of disaster preparedness. What do employees do in case of a fire, electrical shut down, or other unforeseen act of nature? Sexual harassment is also an area that we need to be concerned about. What can we do to ensure the safety of our employees and to avoid liability as owners and managers? While I am not a legal expert in this area, I do recommend the following:

Make sure that the proper health and safety signs are posted in the work or break area. The government mandates many of these notices. If you are not sure which signs should be displayed, contact your local labor board and OSHA. Make sure your coworkers have read them. Most people do not read bulletin boards unless they are looking to buy a used car or looking to rent an apartment. Don't assume because a notice is posted that it will be read or even understood.

Make a list of potential safety problems for your particular business. This list will vary according to the business you are in. It might include some of those I have suggested above. Update the list as your experience with the business grows.

Develop written instructions that clearly outline for coworkers what they should and should not do. Keep the instructions simple but make sure they are complete. For example, what should a coworker do and not do in the case of a robbery, or sexual harassment, or to avoid back injury, or customer injury? This should be an integral part of your training program. Again, do not assume because someone has read instructions that he or she understood them. To reduce future exposure to lawsuits, have coworkers sign a form that indicates they received training in these areas.

Include in your new coworker training a section on health and safety issues. The litigious business environment we are now living in makes this absolutely essential. I have another business associate who owns a number of fast food restaurants. One of his employees sued him because she said she was sexually harassed by one of his managers. He won the lawsuit. Or did he? It cost him $15,000 in legal fees!

Handle Workman's Compensation claims immediately and document everything. Here are some critical questions that need to be answered in writing:

How and when did the coworker get hurt?

What were the injuries?

Were there witnesses?

What happened, step-by-step?

You may also choose, if it is legal in your state, to have a drug test administered to the coworker. Today, it is not uncommon for some injuries to be a result of drug abuse. If coworkers fail the drug test they can be terminated.

You might also videotape the coworker and the place where the accident occurred.

Coworker Theft

Coworker theft costs business owners billions of dollars each year. That's right! I said billions, not millions. It was estimated that in 1995, 40% of all business failures in the United States were because of employee theft. How do we as business owners and managers allow this to happen? For myself, I have always believed that the people I hired were honest. I changed my thinking after one of my managers stole over $2000 from me. How did she do it? She sold product and pocketed the money. I should have been a smarter business owner. This is particularly true because of a lesson I should have learned from my Dad when I was about fifteen.

My Dad owned a very successful meat processing plant and serviced local restaurants with meat products, etc. One evening at about nine o'clock, we went to the plant, entered the back door, and, with the aid of a flashlight, went to the large freezer that held all of the frozen products. My Dad counted all of the boxes and then did a very strange thing. He took a piece of thread out of his pocket, attached it to one side of the door jam and then to the other. We then left the freezer, making sure we stepped over the thread. I had some idea that he was concerned someone was stealing from him. The next morning we went to the plant very early. Dad opened the freezer door and found the thread was broken. He called around and found that his driver was selling product on the side and pocketing the money. The driver was my Dad's very best friend! He had known him for years and had hired him thinking that friends don't steal from friends. Here is the lesson I should have learned. Always assume that employees are stealing. Never assume they are not!

One study of employee theft indicated the following:

- 20 percent of all employees are likely to steal
- 20 percent won't steal no matter what the opportunity
- 60 percent will steal if they find the risk to be minimal

What do employers do to make it easy for employees to steal?:

- They have ineffective security systems

- They have poor controls for handling money and for accounting for inventory
- They have no system for checking on employees

What can we do to minimize employee theft?

First, assume that everyone will steal or cheat if they get the chance. How will they cheat or steal? They will take merchandise and products. They will steal money. They will waste product. They will loaf on the job. They will give customers too much for the price paid.

You should also assume that delivery people might short you on things ordered. Therefore, every delivery should be carefully checked against the invoice.

Second, coworkers and outside help must be carefully monitored. Anyone who has access to money or financial records can be a potential con artist. Bookkeepers can embezzle hundreds of thousands of dollars. Those who prepare bank deposits can steal from you. People become very good at stealing. They falsify records and cover their tracks extremely well.

Third, use a pre-employment honesty test. As indicated before, this test will tell you how likely it is that an employee, if given the opportunity, will steal from you. Honesty tests can be found on the Internet.

Fourth, explain to each employee, at the time of hiring, what your expectations are relative to honesty. This might include specific directions as to food they can eat without charge or discounts they receive as an employee. Also, explain to them the consequences should they be found dishonest.

Fifth, develop systems to check daily inventory that comes in and products that are sold. Most businesses have certain key items that can be checked to determine if what was sold equals the money that was taken in. Modern cash registers and computers now track such things and are well worth the expense.

Sixth, work in the business to insure that the desired results are occurring. Often, it is the absentee owners or the multi-unit owners who are not aware of what is going on in their businesses. Daily spot checks by an owner are essential to discourage theft.

Seventh, should your business be conducive to employee theft, install a video monitoring system. These are available in most areas for a relatively nominal fee. This system is a great deterrent to employee theft and to robbery.

There is one motto every business owner and manager should live by: "If it can happen it will." The problems occur when we assume it will never happen to us! A little planning and prevention up front is worth, as someone said, "a pound of cure later on."

Chapter 14 Summary

- Among a Leader's chief concerns is a safe workplace.

- Leaders anticipate problems before they occur.

- Leaders must be aware not only of the possibility, but the likelihood, of theft and other forms of dishonesty by coworkers.

Chapter 15

Compliance with Business Regulations

Principle: It is better to be safe than sorry.

As we stated at the end of the previous chapter, "An ounce of prevention is worth a pound of cure." This is especially true with regard to litigation in the workplace.

A multitude of federal laws, regulations, and court cases governing every aspect of employment creates a legal minefield for employers, who risk substantial potential liability for failing to stay in compliance. There are also state statutes and regulatory and common law rules that often parallel federal law but differ materially in a number of components. In many cases, state laws are more stringent than federal laws.

The purpose of this chapter is twofold: First, to give you an overview of federally-mandated laws and regulations; and, two, to assist you in reducing as much as possible your exposure to litigation.

The information given here is designed to provide accurate and authoritative information. *However, it should not be relied upon solely nor should it be a substitute for specific legal advice. I am not a lawyer!* There is no single rule or uniform body of legal standards that apply with equal force throughout the country. You are advised to consult competent labor attorneys when evaluating and implementing employment-related policies and procedures. The chapter is divided into 5 sections, each dealing with a specific category of legal concern:

1. Discrimination
2. Health and Safety Issues
3. Administration and Privacy Issues
4. Wage and Hour Issues
5. Hiring and Termination Issues

Discrimination

Equal Employment Opportunity Title VII

Applies to: All employers with more than 15 employees.

Requirements: Prohibits pre-employment questions and/or employment discrimination or harassment on the basis of sex, race, color, religion, or national origin. Employers must have a written EEO policy and a published process by which employees can complain. Employers must reasonably accommodate employees' religious beliefs.

Suggested Actions:

- Employment documents and forms must be in compliance with EEO requirements. Only job-related questions may be asked or required to be answered.

- Issue an employee handbook with a strong and clearly worded anti-discrimination policy that covers all types of discrimination and harassment. Make sure that it is given to every employee and that it contains a clear process by which employees can voice complaints.

- Always use written employment agreements to avoid contractual liability for handbook content.

- Post required posters relating to EEO employment laws.
- Keep all employment records for at least one year after an action.

Sexual Harassment Title VII

Applies to: All employers with more than 15 employees.

Requirements: Prohibits sexual harassment which includes any unwelcome sexual conduct that: a. Establishes a term or condition of an individual's employment or; b. Has the purpose of unreasonably interfering with an individual's work performance or creating an intimidating, hostile, or offensive working environment., or c. Employers may be held liable if they know or should have known of the harassment and failed to take immediate and appropriate corrective action to stop it.

Suggested actions:

- Publish a written sexual harassment policy that includes how an employee may report complaints. The establishment of a clear-cut process is tremendously important: see the phrase "should have known," above.

- Make sure your policy includes employees of the same sex, supervisors, customers, vendors, and other parties' employees may be reluctant to report.

Age Discrimination in Employment

Applies to all employers with over 20 employees.

Requirements: Prohibits discrimination against individuals 40 years of age or older.

Suggested actions:

- Use approved employment applications that do not require age information.
- Do not include age preferences in job or requirement notices.

Americans with Disabilities Act – 1990

Applies to: All employers with more than 15 employees

Requirements: Prohibits discrimination against qualified individuals;

a. Qualified individuals must be considered for the job.
b. Employer has the right to define essential functions of the job.

c. Job descriptions must define job duties, and functions to perform the job.

d. Employer must offer "reasonable accommodation."

e. Medical inquiries may not be made prior to job offer.

Suggested actions:

- Have clearly established written job descriptions for each job.

- Do not ask job applicants about the severity or nature of a disability, only their ability to perform job requirements.

- All applicants may be tested for illegal drug use.

Family and Medical Leave Act (FMLA)

Applies to: All employers with 50 or more employees.

Requirements: Employer must allow employees to take up to 12 weeks of unpaid leave during a 12 month period for birth, adoption, foster care, or for a serious health condition, but may not require employee to disclose the nature of any serious health condition.

Suggested actions:

- Be familiar with local state statutes that cover family leave issues.

- Employees who return from FMLA are entitled to return to the same job or an equivalent job.

Pregnancy Discrimination Act

Applies to: All employers with 15 or more employees.

Requirements: Prohibits discrimination on the basis of pregnancy, childbirth, or related medical conditions. Women who are pregnant are to be treated in the same manner as other temporarily disabled applicants/employees with similar conditions.

Suggested actions:

- Post notices and provide a written policy in the employee handbook that addresses this issue.

Immigration and Nationality Act

Applies to: All employers

Requirements: Requires that employers only hire persons who may legally work in the U.S.; citizens and nationals of the U.S. and authorized aliens. Also prohibits discrimination against individuals on the basis of national origin or citizenship.

Suggested actions:

- Verify the identity and employment eligibility of anyone you hire.
- Complete and retain a Form 1-9 in accordance with its printed instructions.
- Complete Sections 1 and 2 at the time of hire,
- Retain 1-9 forms for 1 year after a person's termination.

Health and Safety Issues

OSHA

Applies to: All employers

Requirements: Work and safety is regulated by the laws of most states and the Federal Occupational Safety and Health Act (OSHA). These require that employers provide places of employment that are free from recognized hazards that can cause illness, death, or serious harm.

Suggested actions:

- Establish a written procedure for ongoing safety training, beginning with the initial training.
- Keep documentation of all employees who attend training sessions.

- Adhere to safety posting procedures.
- Provide employees with procedures and telephone numbers to be used in emergency situations.
- Investigate accidents immediately and advise your safety counselor.

Chemical Hazards-Right to Know

Applies to: All employers

<u>Requirements</u>: Employees have the "right to know" of risks associated with certain hazardous substances to which they may be exposed in the workplace.

Suggested actions:

- Train all employees on chemical safety.
- Report any accidents immediately.

Worker's Compensation

Applies to: Mandated by most states.

<u>Requirements</u>: Assures compensation for medical treatment, rehabilitation expenses, and for lost wages for employees who suffer job-related injury or illness.

Suggested actions:

- Make sure you know that your employees are covered by Worker's Compensation.
- Post required information where employees can see it.
- Employee handbooks and agreements must require employees to report accidents or injuries immediately.
- Require all new hires to complete a medical history questionnaire following a conditional offer of employment.
- Report and treat all employee injuries/accidents immediately.
- Report injuries immediately to your Worker's Compensation agent or carrier.
- File all reports on time.
- Require a doctor's release after an injury.

Workplace Violence

Applies to: All employers

Requirements: Employers can be found liable for actions of their employees if: the employee is acting within the scope of his/her employment, the employee is negligent, and the employee's negligence is the cause of injuries.

Suggested actions:

- Have a written violence prevention policy that communicates to employees that workplace violence will not be tolerated and that offenders will face disciplinary action.

- Implement pre-employment screening and safety training for employees and supervisors.

- Make sure the Employee handbook contains language that requires any workplace violence or threat of violence to be reported immediately. Tell employees where and how to report it.

- The Employee handbook should spell out in clear language what employees are to do in case of robbery or other acts of violence at the workplace.

Drug-Free Workplace

Applies to: No federally mandated requirements, but a great potential liability for business owners.

<u>Requirements</u>: Employers must establish a drug-free awareness program and notify employees of such. Notify employees in writing that, as a condition of employment, they will (1) abide by terms of the policy; (2) notify the employer of a conviction under a drug statute not later than 5 days after conviction. An employer must notify the appropriate agency of the employee conviction within 10 days and within 30 days must either terminate the employee or require participation in a drug rehabilitation program.

Suggested actions:

- Have a written Substance Abuse or Drug and Alcohol policy that prohibits drug and alcohol-related activities, identifies workplace standards and penalties, educates as to the dangers of abuse, announces testing policies, and how to report violations.

- Screening of employees may include questions about current illegal drug use -- not questions about prescription drugs.
- Consult a qualified legal counsel when establishing a drug-testing program.

COBRA Health Insurance Continuation Rights

Applies to: All employers with more than 20 employees.

<u>Requirements</u>: Employer must notify an employee within 14 days of termination or resignation that they are eligible for COBRA insurance coverage. Employee has 60 days to accept.

Suggested actions:

- Does not apply to termination due to gross misconduct.
- Employees can continue coverage up to 18 months.
- Employees must pay premiums and keep them current.
- Termination of health coverage by an employee terminates COBRA obligations of employers.

Administration and Privacy Issues

Right to Privacy

Applies to: All employers.

<u>Requirements</u>: Employee's records are protected from disclosure to third parties.

Suggested actions:

- Obtain written permission from applicants to release information to a third party.

- All medical records are strictly confidential, and are available only on a "need to know" basis.

- Employer can furnish a truthful statement concerning a reason for discharge, or why an employee voluntarily left. Withholding information to a third party about an employee's violent work behavior could make the employer liable.

Tax Code Liabilities

Applies to: All employers.

<u>Requirements</u>: Federal, state and local taxes must be reported and paid on time. Withholding from employee earnings must be done in compliance with statutory requirements. Improper handling of tax reports and/or

payments can be financially devastating, especially the mishandling of Social Security and Medicare monies.

Suggested action:

- Use a qualified accountant and standard accounting practices to document all financial transactions.

Liability Insurance

Applies to: Most business owners.

<u>Requirements</u>: Today's litigious business environment requires employers to protect themselves from potential liability.

Suggested actions:

- Consider obtaining "employment liability insurance" after consultation with qualified advisor.

- Consider coverage that includes discrimination; harassment; negligent hiring; supervision training; wrongful termination; defamation of character; invasion of privacy; and customer injury.

Fair Credit Reporting Act (FCRA)

Applies to: All employers.

<u>Requirements</u>: Affords privacy and protects individuals from adverse action that may result from inaccurate information contained in background checks.

Suggested actions:

- Always obtain a written release that permits you to conduct background checks.

<u>Wage and Hour Issues</u>

Wage and Hour-Fair Labor Standards (FLSA)

Applies to: All employers.

<u>Requirements</u>: Employers must pay federally mandated minimum wage and must post conspicuously the U.S. Department of Labor WH Publication 1088. Employers must pay overtime for hours worked over 40 per week.

Suggested actions:

- The Employee Handbook needs to clearly explain personnel practices such as overtime pay, bonuses, uniform requirements, hours of work, etc.
- Check with state regulations to see if they are higher than FLSA.

- Post all documents required by FLSA.

Hiring and Termination Issues

Wrongful Discharge

Applies to: All employers.

Requirements: While most employment is at-will, employers are generally held to a stricter standard of fairness and conduct with long-term employees. Discharged employees may file a wrongful termination complaint separate and apart from any other discrimination or other statutory claims.

Suggested action:

- Employment application, handbooks and agreements should contain an at-will employment relationship.

- It is not required for you to give a reason for termination when an at-will relationship is in place, but if a reason is obvious, it should be well documented and for good cause.

- At-will terminations will not relieve you of potential unemployment claims.

- Do not terminate based on unproved allegations of a third party, even if you believe them to be true.

Breach of Employment Contract

Applies to: All employers.

<u>Requirements</u>: Employers can be held liable for oral or written statements that imply a contract relationship with an employee.

Suggested actions:

- Do not hire anyone without executing an employment agreement that contains "at-will" language.
- Make sure that terms and conditions of employment in employee handbooks are consistent with current employment agreements.
- Make sure that Employment Agreements and handbooks are not changed without your review and consent.
- Make no statements that are contrary to employment "at-will."

Negligent Hiring, Supervision and Retention

Applies to: All private employers.

Requirements: Employers will be held liable for hiring unsuitable employees, or a failure to supervise that results in injury to customers, clients or fellow employees. Employers can require background checks including social security, criminal history, but not medical history.

Suggestion actions:

- Ask all references the same job-related questions, including questions about attendance, substance abuse, workplace violence, reprimands, reason for termination.

Unemployment Insurance

Applies to: All employers.

Requirements: While employment "at-will" permits employers to terminate with or without advance notice, for good cause or no good cause, it does not permit termination for wrong or bad cause, based on state or common law. Violation of state common law may result in award of unemployment insurance payments for an employee wrongfully terminated. Employees can receive unemployment if they quit for good cause.

Suggested action:

- Use the employment "at-will" relationship for terminating only those employees whose unacceptable behavior causes severe or continued damage to the business.
- Document all disciplinary actions of an employee and keep these in employment files to show cause for termination.
- Obtain a signed statement of reason for termination at the exit interview.
- Have a witness who can substantiate the reason stated for termination if the employee refuses to sign the document.
- Comply with state unemployment information requests in a timely manner.
- Challenge any unwarranted claims with an explanation and documentation of facts.

Regulations Checklist

This chapter should be reviewed a number of times by business owners and managers. To assist you, the following checklist reviews the major things you must do to be in compliance with the regulations reviewed in this chapter. Check each one "yes" or "no". You will then have a good indication of the areas you need to focus on.

Discrimination Issues

Yes   No

___   ___   1. In interviews do you only ask job related questions, avoiding those that deal with sex, race, color, religion, or national origin?

___   ___   2. Do you use an Employment Application form that has been reviewed by a competent Labor Lawyer?

___   ___   3. Do you avoid asking candidates about the severity or nature of disabilities, focusing only on their ability to perform job requirements?

___   ___   4. Do you make sure not to include age requirements in job notices?

Screening Candidates

___   ___   5. Do you make job offers conditional upon the results of background checks and a medical questionnaire?

___ ___ 6. Do you always obtain a written release permitting you to conduct background checks?

___ ___ 7. Do you complete at the time of hire and retain in a file I-9 forms for each employee?

___ ___ 8. Do you retain I-9 forms for 1 year after termination of an employee?

___ ___ 9. Do you obtain a current DMV report for each employee who will drive?

___ ___ 10. Do you screen candidates for pervious workplace violence?

___ ___ 11. Do you screen for illegal drug use?

Employee Handbook – Do you have an employee handbook that:

___ ___ 12. Is in compliance with EEO requirements -- strongly worded ant-discrimination and sexual harassment policies?

___ ___ 13. Clearly explains to employees what to do if they have a complaint?

___ ___ 14. Clearly describes job requirements for each position?

___ ___ 15. Tells employees how to report injuries?

___ ___ 16. Tells employees what to do in case of workplace violence?

___ ___ 17. Outlines Substance Abuse or Drug and Alcohol standards and testing?

___ ___ 18. Clearly explains personnel practices such as overtime pay, bonuses, and uniform requirements?

___ ___ 19. Contains an at-will employment relationship?

___ ___ 20. Is consistent in terms and conditions with the employee agreement?

Health and Safety

___ ___ 21. Do you have a safety training program, with procedures for on-going safety training?

___ ___ 22. Do you keep records on all employees who attend safety training?

___ ___ 23. You have a first aid kit available for employees?

___ ___ 24. Does each employee have a written procedure for what to do in emergency situations, along with telephone numbers of whom to contact?

___ ___ 25. Do you investigate accidents immediately and report them?

___ ___ 26. Are you informed as to local safety regulations?

___ ___ 27. Do you train all employees on chemical safety, if such are used?

___ ___ 28. Do you provide accident-reporting procedures for drivers?

___ ___ 29. Are all drivers trained on defensive and bad weather driving?

___ ___ 30. Do you notify employees, within 14 days, of termination, of COBRA rights?

Administrative and Privacy Issues

___   ___   31. Do you obtain written permission from employees to release information to a third party?

___   ___   32. Do you use a qualified accountant to document all financial transactions?

___   ___   33. Do you have all of the insurance coverage necessary?

___   ___   34. Have you considered employer liability insurance?

___   ___   35. Have you conferred with an attorney or accountant to determine the best legal structure for your business?

Wage and Hour Issues

___   ___   36. Have you reviewed state wage and hour regulations to insure that you are in compliance?

Hiring and Termination Issues

___   ___   37. Have all employees signed a current employment agreement?

___   ___   38. Does your employment agreement contain the following

- an at-will employment relationship
- a statement that there has been no contractual relationship implied in any written materials or in verbal communications

- an authorization to conduct background checks
- trade secret and unfair competition protection?

___   ___   39. Do you document all disciplinary actions with employees and keep them in the employee's file?

___   ___   40. Do you obtain a signed statement of reason for termination from employees?

___   ___   41. Do you treat pregnant employees as temporarily disabled employees?

___   ___   42. Is your health insurance for all employees in compliance with state regulations?

Posting Requirements- Do you have the following posted in places visible to employees?

___   ___   43. Equal Employment Opportunity?

___   ___   44. Pregnancy Discrimination Act?

___   ___   45. Safety procedures with emergency telephone numbers?

___   ___   46. Workmen's Compensation?

___   ___   47. Wage and Hour-Fair Labor Standards?

Chapter 15 Summary

- Business managers must be aware of state and federal regulations governing hiring, safety, training, and termination of coworkers.

- Seek the advice of competent lawyers and accountants.

- Liability insurance is essential in today's business environment.

- Make sure that all required notices are properly posted and understood by coworkers.

Conclusion

A principle is a truth that can light our way and govern our conduct in an infinite number of like situations. It's like a good tool, something to keep ready at hand. Like tools, the truth and value of a principle is proven over time in the experience of those who use it in their lives. How do we know they're true? Simply because they <u>work</u>!

So, having finished this book, you're probably wondering if there's not some principle of success in management that underlies all other principles featured here, that is, a sort of primary truth or universal principle that makes one a leader.

I believe there is such a principle. It's best illustrated in a fable told by Aesop, a wise old Greek who is said to have lived six centuries before the birth of Jesus Christ.

In Aesop's fable the sun and the wind, two powerful forces of nature, were arguing about which of them was the more powerful. The sun boasted of its withering heat, the wind of its hurricane force. The debate between the two had been going on for some time when both noticed a lone man walking along the road below. The man was bundled up in a greatcoat against the weather, which was rather blustery and chill. "Ah," said the wind, "look at that man. He gathers his coat around him, but I tell you I can blow it off him with a good thunderous blast."

"Hah," said the sun, unconvinced by the wind's boasting. "Give it a try."

So the wind blew and blew—not just a stiff wind but a gale force. Yet the more the wind blew, the tighter the man pulled his coat around him. In such a wind, the man could hardly stand upright, but the wind failed to blow the coat from the man and soon gave up, defeated and disgusted.

Now it was the sun's turn. "Watch my power," he said.

The sun first warmed the air, the sun's rays falling gently on the man, who began to perspire under all that heavy cloth. As the temperature increased, the man unbuttoned the coat and soon slung it over his shoulder and continued walking down the road. The sun had won the contest. His gentleness had triumphed over force.

In managing people, as we have seen, it is always tempting to use the cattle prod approach. Aren't we, after all, in charge? And don't we have the power to hire, discipline, and fire?

The answer to both of these questions is, of course, you bet! But our power is an illusion if we believe that we can secure the cooperation of our coworkers through the stiff winds and gales of coercion. That was the wind's mistake. It's also the mistake of the Drill Sergeant, who confuses leadership with command. Aesop's fable teaches us otherwise. The sun, finally, was more powerful than the wind because he was a better psychologist (he knew how the old man would respond) , a better communicator, (he sent the right message) , and a better manager (he got the results both wanted).

To anyone skeptical about this or any other management principle I've used in this book I say only, "Hey, don't take my word for it. Give the principle a try. If the principle fails to bring you the desired results, then find some other principle—one that works for you."

I think your experimentation will turn out otherwise, however, and you'll be pleased to find that the principles put forth here are not only true, they work. I hope they work for you and the coworkers you LEAD.

INDEX